CONTENTS

KT-457-653

HOW TO USE THIS BOOK 4

THE AGE OF THE EARTH 6
• Oldest minerals, rocks and meteorites • The Precambrian eon
• Phanerozoic eon to present day • Major events • Previous estimates
of the age of the Earth • Geological timescale

PLATE TECTONICS 8
• Continental drift • Seafloor spreading • Another theory
• Some speeds • Features of the Earth caused by plate movement
• Cross section of the Earth

ROCKS & MINERALS 10
• Types of rock • Sediments to sedimentary rock • Examples of igneous
rock • Examples of sedimentary rock • The rock cycle • Examples of
Metamorphic rock

FOSSILS 12
• How fossils form • The uses of fossils • Before fossilization
• During fossilization • Fossil assemblages • After fossilization

PRECAMBRIAN 14
• Precambrian world • Stromatolites • Vendian period
• Snowball Earth • Animals of the Vendian

EARLY PALAEOZOIC 16
• Palaeozoic era • Land animals • Cambrian • Ordovician • Silurian
• The Burgess Shale • Calymene • Diplograptus

DEVONIAN 18
• The world in the Devonian • Plants • The age of fishes
• Changing atmosphere • Old red sandstone • Cephalaspis
• Eusthenopteron • Ichthyostega

CARBONIFEROUS 20
• The world in the Carboniferous • One period or two?
• Formation of coal • Coal forest plants • Eogyrinus • Meganeura
• Westlothiana

PERMIAN 22
• The world in the Permian • Desert features • Reefs
• Mesosaurus • Pareiasaurus • Dimetrodon

TRIASSIC 24
• The world in the Triassic • Mesozoic era • Glossopteris
• Meaning of the name • New plant life
• Reasons for the mass extinction • Triassic climates

TRIASSIC LIFE 26
• Changing plants, changing animals • Hard-shelled egg — the key
to land-living • Footprints • What makes a dinosaur? • Eoraptor
• Thecodontosaurus • Eudimorphodon

JURASSIC 28
• The world in the Jurassic • Mass extinctions • Meaning of the name
• Typical Jurassic rocks • Two Jurassic rock sequences • Economic
importance • Index fossils

JURASSIC LIFE 30
• The life on a continental shelf • Cryptoclidus
• The fossils of the lagoons • Liopleurodon
• Pterodactylus

JURASSIC DINOSAURS 32
• Dinosaur types • A dinosaur landscape • Stegosaurus
• Diplodocus

CRETACEOUS 34
• The world in the Cretaceous • Diverse dinosaurs
• Meaning of the name • Tylosaurus • Animals of air and sea
• Elasmosaurus • Kronosaurus • Arambourgiana

CRETACEOUS LIFE 36
• Saltasaurus • Caudipteryx • Velociraptor • Tyrannosaurus •
Therizinosaurus• Carnotaurus

CREACEOUS PLANT-EATERS 38
• New plants • Varied habitats • Iguanodon • Parasaurolophus •
Euoplocephalus • Triceratops

THE GREAT EXTINCTION 40
• What caused the Great Extinction? • Diseases
• Meteorite or comet strike • Changing climates • Volcanic activity
• A combination of all of these • Winners and losers • Repenomamus

EARLY TERTIARY 42
• The world in the Early Tertiary • Plant and animal life • Meaning of
the name • Mammal names • Brontotherium • Hyracotherium
• Diatryma • Oxyaena

LATE TERTIARY 44
• The world in the Late Tertiary • Phorusrhacos • The coming of grass
• Deinotherium • Synthetoceras • Sivatherium
• Cooling climate

QUATERNARY 46
• The world in the Quaternary • Causes of the Ice Age • Meaning of the
name • Ages of the Quaternay • Glacial stages • Evidence of glaciation
• Smilodon • Elephas Primigenius • Megatherium • Macrauchenia

THE FIRST HUMANS 48
• When and where did humans first appear? • Why did we stand
upright? • Orrorin • Ardipithecus • Kenyanthropus
• Australopithecus

THE GENUS HOMO 50
• Out of the cradle • The development of culture and civilization
• Homo

UNCOVERING THE PREHISTORIC WORLD 52
• Timeline of the History of Geology and Palaeontology • Some wrong
deductions

KEY FIGURES 54

PALAEONTOLOGY 56
• Dinosaurs all around the world • Finding dinos • Excavation and
transportation • In the lab • Dino displays • Museums with good
dinosaur collections

GLOSSARY 58

INDEX 60

HOW TO USE THIS BOOK

JUST THE FACTS, THE PREHISTORIC WORLD is an easy-to-use, quick way to look up facts about dinosaurs, early reptiles, amphibians and mammals. Every page is packed with names, statistics and key pieces of information about the history of Earth. For fast access to *just the facts*, follow the tips on these pages.

TIMELINES
A breakdown of the names given to the different subdivisions of time.

BOX HEADINGS
Look for heading words linked to your research to guide you to the right fact box.

INTRODUCTION TO TOPIC

TWO QUICK WAYS TO FIND A FACT:

1 Look at the detailed **CONTENTS** list on page 3 to find your topic of interest.

CONTENTS

...entary rock • The rock cyc...
...ssils form • The uses of fossils • Before fossilization
...ing fossilization • Fossil assemblages • After fossilization

RECAMBRIAN 14
Precambrian world • Stromatolites • Vendian period
Snowball Earth • Animals of the Vendian

EARLY PALAEOZOIC 16
• Palaeozoic era • Land animals • Cambrian • Ordovician • Silurian
The Burgess Shale • Calymene • Diplograptus

DEVONIAN 18
...the world in the Devonian • Plants • The age of fishes
...anging atmosphere • Old red sandstone • Cephalaspis
...enopteron • Ichthyostega

...NIFEROUS ....
...the Carboniferous • One period or two?
...Coal forest plants • Eogyrinus • M...

Turn to the relevant page and use the **BOX HEADINGS** to find the information box you need.

2 Turn to the **INDEX** which starts on page 60 and search for key words relating to your research.
• The index will direct you to the correct page, and where on the page to find the fact you need.

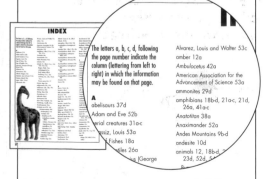

INDEX

The letters a, b, c, d, following the page number indicate the column (lettering from left to right) in which the information may be found on that page.

A
abelisaurs 37d
Adam and Eve 52b
...rial creatures 31a-c
...ssiz, Louis 53a
...f Fishes 18a
...tiles 26a
...us (George

Alvarez, Louis and Walter 53c
amber 12a
Ambulocetus 42a
American Association for the Advancement of Science 53a
ammonites 29d
amphibians 18b-d, 21a-c, 21d, 26a, 41a-c
Anatotitan 38a
Anaximander 52a
Andes Mountains 9b-d
andesite 10d
animals 12, 18b-d, 21a-c, 23d, 52d, 5...
Bu...

EARLY PALAEOZOIC

EARLY PALAEOZOIC TIMELINE

543-417 MYA

	Silurian	Pridoli
		Ludlow
		Wenlock
Early Palaeozoic		Llandovery
	Ordovician	Bala
		Dyfed
		Canadian
	Cambrian	Merioneth
		St David's
		Caerfai

During this time, our film of the Earth's history is starting to get exciting. However, nearly all the action takes place at the bottom of the sea. All sorts of hard-shelled animals have evolved by this time and all the main groups that exist today had come into being. By the end of this section, life was beginning to quit the waters and come out on to land.

PALAEOZOIC ERA

The Palaeozoic era is made up of six periods.
The first three make up the early Palaeozoic period and the other three are the Devonian, Carboniferous and the Permian.

Permian 290-248

Carboniferous 354-290

Devonian 417-354

Early Palaeozoic 543-417

LAND ANIMALS

Although we say that there were no land animals in the early Palaeozoic, we know of some strange trace fossils from Canada, from the Cambrian period. They were made by a soft-bodied animal. The flat-bodied animal hauled itself along the damp sand of the Cambrian shoreline. The animal had flaps on either side of its body and dug those into the sand to pull itself forward, creating tracks that look like motorcycle tracks.

SILURIAN PERIOD 443-417

Meaning: From Silures — an old Welsh tribe.
Continents were continuing to move together. The edges of the continents were flooded, giving large areas of shallow sea over continental shelves. Many reefs and shallow-water organisms existed at that time. The first land-living plants appeared.

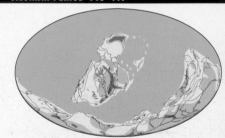

ORDOVICIAN PERIOD 490-443

Meaning: From Ordovices — an old Welsh tribe.
In the Ordovician period the northern landmasses were beginning to move towards one another. An ice age took place at the boundary with the Silurian, 450 to 440 million years ago.

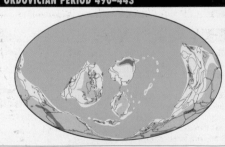

CAMBRIAN 543-490

Meaning: From Cambria — an old name for Wales, where the original work was done on the lower Palaeozoic rocks.
In the early Palaeozoic all of the southern continents — South America, Africa, India, Australia and Antarctica — were part of a single landmass. The northern continents — North America, Europe and Asia — were individual landmasses scattered over the ocean.

16

JUST THE FACTS
Each topic box presents the facts you need in short, quick-to-read points.

52-53 Uncovering the Prehistoric World Timeline

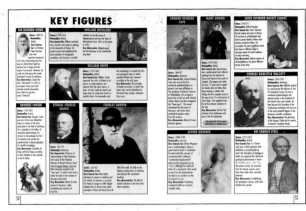

54-55 Key Figure Biographies

THE BURGESS SHALE

The most spectacular set of Cambrian fossils lies in the Burgess Shale in Canada. These consist of all kinds of animals, most of which don't seem to fit into any established classification. It is as if nature were trying out every shape imaginable as soon as hard animal parts had evolved, just to see what would work and what would not.

Burgess shale animals
Marella – like a trilobite with long horns on its head.
Nectocaris – like a shrimp's body with an eel's tail.
Opabinia – like a worm with a trunk and many pairs of paddles.
Wiwaxia – like a slug covered in chain mail.

Hallucigenia – a worm-like body with tentacles along one side and stilts along the other.
Anomalocaris – a big swimming predator that probably hunted all these.

See page 55 for more information on Charles Doolittle Walcott who discovered the Burgess Shale.

The Burgess Shale in Canada today.

CALYMENE

Time: Silurian
Size: About 3 cm (1 3/16 in)
Diet: Organic particles from sea bed
Habitat: Shallow seas
Information: *Calymene* was a typical trilobite — one of the most abundant of the sea-living arthropods in the early Paleozoic.

Pygidium – tail shield made from fused segments
Thorax – central part of body made up of segments
Cephalon – head shield

DIPLOGRAPTUS

Time: Silurian
Size: 5 cm (2 in) each branch
Diet: Suspended organic particles
Habitat: Open water
Information: *Diplograptus* was a common graptolite — a floating colonial organism. It consisted of two rows of living creatures back to back, and several hanging suspended from a gas float.

Other graptolites include *Monograptus*, with a single row of individuals, and *Didymograptus*, with two rows arranged in a wishbone shape. These are all valuable index fossils for the early Paleozoic.

See pages 12-13 for more information on index fossils.

ANIMAL PROFILES

Isotelus
Period: Silurian
Diet: Buried organic matter
Habitat: In sandy sea bottoms
Information: Spade-shaped trilobite, smooth surface, adapted for burrowing.

Eodiscus
Period: Cambrian
Diet: Floating organic matter
Habitat: Open water
Information: Tiny early trilobite, free swimming, only two segments in the thorax, cephalon the same size as pygidium.

Olenellus
Period: Cambrian
Diet: Organic detritus
Habitat: Shallow sea bed
Information: An early trilobite, tiny pygidium, spines on the segments.

Cryptolithus
Period: Ordovician
Diet: Floating organic matter
Habitat: Open water
Information: Free-swimming trilobite, huge cephalon with long spines at the rear, small thorax and pygidium.

17

PICTURE CAPTIONS
Captions explain what is in the pictures.

ANIMAL PROFILES
Different animals' statistics are listed here.

For fast access to facts about different animals, look for the name in the headings.

Isotelus

GLOSSARY
• A GLOSSARY of words and terms used in this book begins on page 58. The glossary words provide additional information to supplement the facts on the main pages.

LINKS
Look for the purple links throughout the book. Each link gives details of other pages where related or additional facts can be found.

See pages 12-13 for more information on index fossils.

ANIMAL FEATURES
A more detailed study of an animal of the time. A picture accompanies the information to give a better idea of what life was like at that time.

The Precambrian eon covers three eras and the greatest expanse of time - over 4000 million years. We only have two pages devoted to this period as primitive lifeforms were only starting to develop over millions of years.

Proterozoic 2500-543 MYA
Archaean 3800-2500 MYA
Hadean 4500-3800 MYA

What the surface of the Earth may have looked like when it was still forming in the Hadean era.

THE AGE OF THE EARTH

A cinema film runs at 24 frames per second. Every second you watch a film, 24 separate pictures flash before your eyes. Now, imagine that the Earth's history is recorded on film, with each year occupying a frame; 24 years will go by in a second. The running time of the film would be something like six years. A truly epic film! Take your seats. Let us sit in our cinema and run it through.

Early Paleozoic 543-417   **Devonian 417-354**   **Carboniferous 354-290**   **Permian 290-248**   **Triassic 248-206**

The first reptiles
In the Carboniferous period, life on land was fully established. The coal forests teem with giant insects and the first reptiles. The forests eventually formed the coal we use as fuel today.

First signs of life on land
In the Early Palaeozoic period, life was predominantly sea-based. Hard-shelled animals were evolving at this time and by the end of the period, life was starting to venture onto the land.

The reptiles flourish
Inbetween the Permian and Triassic periods there was another mass extinction. This brought about a spurt in the development of lifeforms and the first dinosaurs appeared on Earth.

The age of dinosaurs begins
Dinosaurs evolved in the late Triassic period and ruled the Earth until the end of the Cretaceous period. As the continents moved apart, newer and more fantastic dinosaurs evolved on the separate continents.

HOW DO WE KNOW?

We can look at radioactive minerals in rocks.

Radioactive minerals change at a regular rate over time. By looking at the amount of radioactive mineral that has changed, we can work out how long the changes have been going on, and so the length of time since the mineral was formed.

OLDEST MINERALS, ROCKS AND METEORITES

The oldest minerals – 4.3 billion years old, were found in much younger sedimentary rocks in Australia.

The oldest rocks – 4.03 billion years old found in the Great Slave Lake in northwestern Canada (shown below). These are metamorphic rocks and so are formed from rocks that already existed and must have been older.

The oldest meteorites, assumed to have formed at the same time as Earth – 4.6 billion years ago.

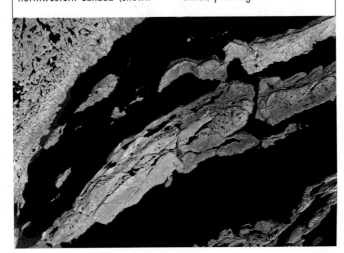

PREVIOUS ESTIMATES OF THE AGE OF THE EARTH

- **About 5 or 6 thousand years** – going by the dates in the Bible, and universally accepted until about 150 years ago.

- **25 – 40 million years – Lord Kelvin in 1862**. He based his calculation on how long the Earth would take to cool to its present temperature assuming that it came into being hot and molten. He did not know about radioactivity that continues to generate heat and so the Earth cools much more slowly.

- **Irish Geologist Samuel Haughton in 1878** suggested that the age could be estimated by measuring the depth of sedimentary rocks.

- **27.6 million years – Walcott in 1893**.

- **18.3 million years – Sollas in 1900**. Both he and Walcott were influenced by Haughton.

- **704 million years – Goodchild in 1897**.

- **96 million years – John Joly in 1889**. He was working on the rate of buildup of salt in the ocean.

Jurassic 206-144   Cretaceous 144-65

The Great Extinction
At the end of the Cretaceous period, a cataclysmic event occured which wiped out all the dinosaurs, pterosaurs and sea reptiles. This cleared the way for the first mammals: our ancient ancestors.

The age of mammals
After nearly all of life is wiped out by the Great Extinction, the Early Tertiary period sees life on Earth taking a new direction. Gone are the dinosaurs and great pterosaurs that ruled the sky, new creatures that graze on the newly developing grass and plants thrive during this time.

Man first appears
Man first appeared only at the very last part of this film. If this film takes six years to watch, human history will take up three and a half minutes of screen time, and your life will flash by in about three seconds.

PHANEROZOIC EON TO PRESENT DAY

The Phanerozoic eon also covers three eras: The Paleozoic which is highlighted in **GREEN**, The Mesozoic highlighted in **PURPLE** and the Cenozoic which is in **RED**. Each one of these are then subdivided into different times, as shown in the film. Although the Phanerozoic eon is only 543 million years, it covers the period when life advances on Earth, which is why the vast majority of this book is devoted to this period.

GEOLOGICAL TIME SCALE

- When the geological time scale is shown vertically the oldest division is always at the bottom and the youngest, or the present day, is at the top.
- This reflects the sequence in which sedimentary rocks are laid down (see p10-11).

7

PLATE TECTONICS

I n 1492, Christopher Columbus sailed the Atlantic and became the first European recorded to have set foot in North America. His voyage took him 70 days. Had it taken place today it would have taken a little longer because the Atlantic Ocean is some 10 metres (over 30 feet) wider now than it was 500 years ago. The movement that brought this about is the kind of thing that we would be able so see happening while watching our six-year-long cinema film.

CONTINENTAL DRIFT

Look at a map of the world. The shape of the east coast of South America fits into the west coast of Africa. People in the past have noticed this as well.

Francis Bacon in 1620 noticed the similarity but did not suggest a reason.

P Placet in 1668 suggested that the Biblical Flood had forced the continents apart.

Antonio Snider in 1855 drew maps to illustrate how the world used

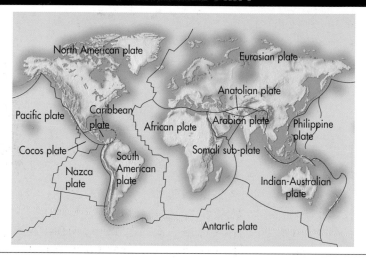

to be, but nobody took him seriously.

FB Taylor in 1908 tried to explain it, along with the formation of mountains, by a movement of continents southwards from the North Pole.

Alfred Wegener in 1915 is credited with beginning the serious scientific discussion of the phenomenon.

See page 55 for more information on Alfred Wegener.

SEAFLOOR SPREADING

- If the continents are moving apart, then something must be happening to the ocean floor inbetween them. Scientists started thinking about this in the late 20th century.

- The crew of the *US Atlantis,* in 1947, noticed that sediment was thin on the floor of the Atlantic Ocean. This meant that part of the ocean floor was younger than other parts.

- Various oceanographic surveys in the 1950s observed oceanic ridges, particularly the one which ran up the centre of the Atlantic.

- American geologist Harry Hess noted in 1960, that the sediment was thinner over the ocean ridges than in the deeper waters at each side. Therefore the ridges were younger than the rest of the ocean.

- British geophysicists Fred Vine

The Azores are a group of islands that lie on the Mid-Atlantic ridge, which were formed by molten rock as the plates moved away from each other.

and Drummond Matthews found, in 1963, that the rocks of the ridges were arranged in strips, magnetized in different directions. They had formed at different times when the Earth's magnetic field was pointing in different directions.

- Canadian geologist Lawrence Morley made the same observations in the Pacific Ocean in 1963.

- Altogether this showed that the oceans were growing larger from their ridges. Volcanic activity formed new seafloor there, and this moved away from the ridge as even newer material formed inbetween. Hess proposed the name "seafloor spreading".

- Put the old idea of continental drift together with the more modern idea of seafloor spreading and we get plate tectonics.

- The surface of the globe is made up of plates, like the panels of a soccer ball. Each panel is growing from a seam along one side, moving along and being swallowed up beneath the next at the seam on the other side. The continents are embedded in these panels and are carried along like logs frozen in ice.

- As the continents move about, they occasionally crash into one another. This causes crumpling up at the edges, forming mountains; fusing together to form bigger continents; or splitting apart as new seams grow beneath them.

- All the continents consist of ancient cores, that have been there for billions of years, and surrounded by progressively younger ranges of mountains.

German geologist OW Hilgenberg and British physicist PAM Dirac (in the 1930s) and British geologist HG Owen (in the 1960s) suggested that the continents were moving apart because the Earth was expanding. Few scientists accept this idea today.

SOME SPEEDS

- Movement of plates in North Atlantic – 2 cm ($\frac{6}{8}$ in) per year. This is typical.

- Movement of plates in Pacific – 4 cm (1 $\frac{5}{8}$ in) per year. This is the fastest.

FEATURES OF THE EARTH CAUSED BY PLATE MOVEMENT

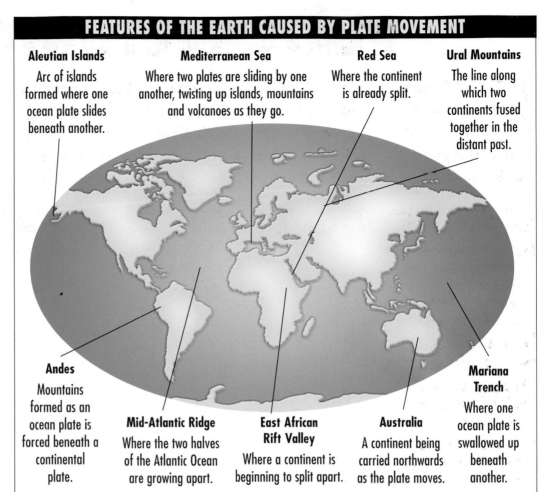

Aleutian Islands
Arc of islands formed where one ocean plate slides beneath another.

Mediterranean Sea
Where two plates are sliding by one another, twisting up islands, mountains and volcanoes as they go.

Red Sea
Where the continent is already split.

Ural Mountains
The line along which two continents fused together in the distant past.

Andes
Mountains formed as an ocean plate is forced beneath a continental plate.

Mid-Atlantic Ridge
Where the two halves of the Atlantic Ocean are growing apart.

East African Rift Valley
Where a continent is beginning to split apart.

Australia
A continent being carried northwards as the plate moves.

Mariana Trench
Where one ocean plate is swallowed up beneath another.

CROSS SECTION OF THE EARTH

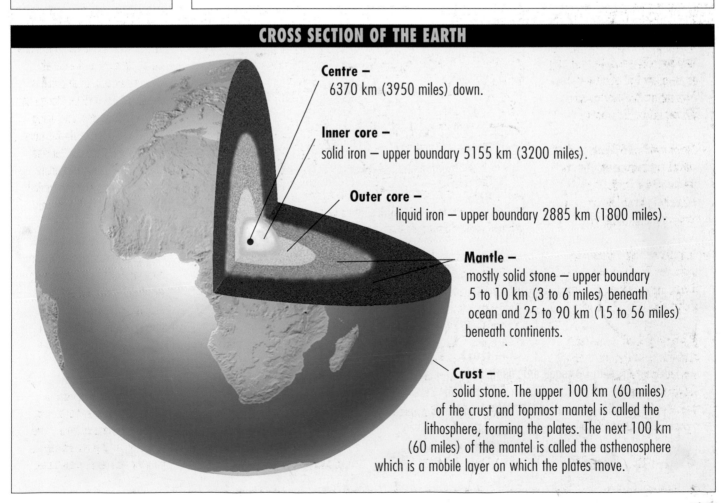

Centre –
6370 km (3950 miles) down.

Inner core –
solid iron – upper boundary 5155 km (3200 miles).

Outer core –
liquid iron – upper boundary 2885 km (1800 miles).

Mantle –
mostly solid stone – upper boundary 5 to 10 km (3 to 6 miles) beneath ocean and 25 to 90 km (15 to 56 miles) beneath continents.

Crust –
solid stone. The upper 100 km (60 miles) of the crust and topmost mantel is called the lithosphere, forming the plates. The next 100 km (60 miles) of the mantle is called the asthenosphere which is a mobile layer on which the plates move.

ROCKS & MINERALS

The crust of the Earth is made up of minerals – substances of a particular chemical combination. Usually minerals form crystals of a particular shape, but sometimes these crystals are distorted or too small to see. When different minerals form together, the result is rock. Minerals and rocks are the film stock from which our epic film is made.

TYPES OF ROCK

There are three types of rock, and these form in different ways.

Igneous rock. This is formed when molten material from inside the Earth cools and solidifies. Usually the minerals can be seen as distinct crystals in igneous rock. There are two types of igneous rock:

A. Intrusive – formed under the surface of the Earth. This tends to be coarse with big crystals.

Intrusive rock

Extrusive rock

B. Extrusive – formed at the surface of the Earth as molten lava from a volcano cools. This is usually fine, with crystals that cannot be seen with the naked eye.

Sedimentary rock. This is formed from fragments that are laid down as layers, or beds. There are three types of sedimentary rock:

A. Clastic – formed from bits of rock that have broken from rocks that already exist.

B. Biogenic – formed from material gathered by living things.

C. Chemical – formed as minerals crystallize out of seawater.

Metamorphic rock. This is the result of already existing rocks being

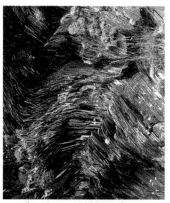
Metamorphic rock

Sedimentary rock

heated and compressed by Earth movements to such an extent that their minerals change. The important thing is that the original rock does not melt – otherwise the result would be an igneous rock. There are two types of metamorphic rock:

A. Thermal metamorphic – formed principally by the action of heat.

B. Regional metamorphic – formed principally by the action of pressure.

SEDIMENTS TO SEDIMENTARY ROCK

Sediments pile up in beds on the bottom of a river, or a sea or a lake, or even in a desert.

- The weight of the beds on top compress those below.
- Ground water percolates through the beds, depositing minerals as it goes, cementing the sedimentary particles together.
- The result is a solid mass – a sedimentary rock.

In any undisturbed sequence the oldest sedimentary bed is at the bottom – hence the convention that is repeated in the geological time scale diagram.

EXAMPLES OF IGNEOUS ROCK

- **Granite** (intrusive) has big crystals through cooling slowly and is light in colour because of the high proportion of silica in the minerals. It comes from deep in mountain ranges.

- **Gabbro** (intrusive) has big crystals and is dark in colour because of the low proportion of silica in the minerals. It is found deep in mountain ranges or the crust of the ocean.

- **Dolerite** (intrusive) is cooled near the surface, so it has smaller crystals – maybe too small to be seen without a microscope.

- **Basalt** (extrusive) is very fine-grained because of rapid cooling as it is solidified lava flow. It has a black colour because of the low proportion of silica minerals. It comes from freely-flowing volcanoes like the ones on Hawaii or Iceland.

- **Andesite** (extrusive) This is very fine-grained because of rapid cooling as it is solidified lava flow. It has a pale colour because of high proportion of silica minerals. It is found in explosive volcanoes like Mount Saint Helens or Vesuvius.

Granite

EXAMPLES OF SEDIMENTARY ROCK

Conglomerate (clastic) is coarse, like a solidified pebble bed and is formed from shingle beaches.

Sandstone (clastic) is medium-grained and formed from sand accumulated in river beds or in deserts.

Shale (clastic) is fine-grained and formed from mud laid down in very thin beds in a river, lake or sea.

Mudstone (clastic) is fine-grained like shale, but does not split into even beds.

Clay (clastic) is so fine-grained that it is difficult to see the fragments, even with a microscope. It is usually formed in still waters like lakes.

Coal (biogenic) is formed as vegetable material piles up in beds and does not rot away.

Halite/rock salt (chemical) is formed as salty waters dry out in lakes or in sheltered bays.

Limestone can be clastic – from previously-formed limestone; biogenic – from seashells or coral reefs; or

chemical – from dissolved calcite in sea water.

Sedimentary rocks are important for fossil formation.

Conglomerate

THE ROCK CYCLE

The material of the Earth's crust is constantly changing, usually through plate-tectonic activity.

Rocks melt and are solidified as igneous rocks. These may break down when exposed and become sedimentary rocks, or may be changed into metamorphic rocks. These then may break down again. This is known as the rock cycle.

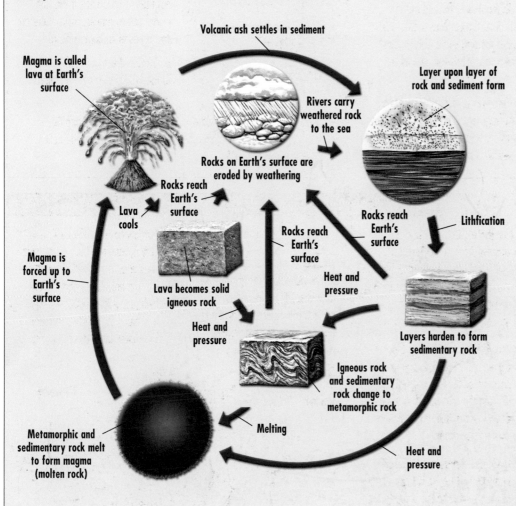

Volcanic ash settles in sediment

Magma is called lava at Earth's surface

Rivers carry weathered rock to the sea

Layer upon layer of rock and sediment form

Rocks on Earth's surface are eroded by weathering

Rocks reach Earth's surface

Lava cools

Rocks reach Earth's surface

Rocks reach Earth's surface

Lithfication

Magma is forced up to Earth's surface

Lava becomes solid igneous rock

Heat and pressure

Heat and pressure

Layers harden to form sedimentary rock

Igneous rock and sedimentary rock change to metamorphic rock

Metamorphic and sedimentary rock melt to form magma (molten rock)

Melting

Heat and pressure

EXAMPLES OF METAMORPHIC ROCK

- **Marble** (thermal) is formed as limestone is cooked by igneous activity.

- **Slate** (regional) is formed as mountain-building activities act on sedimentary rocks like shale. It splits easily along lines of weakness.

- **Schist** (regional) is formed by more intense mountain-building activities. New minerals are formed along twisted bands.

- **Gneiss** (regional) is formed in the extreme depths of mountains and has big obvious crystals.

Gneiss

FOSSILS

We know that animals and plants existed long ago on the Earth. They have left their remains behind as fossils. These may be parts of the original organisms or the traces that they left behind. We can regard the fossils as the inks that form the images on our cinema film – images that allow us to observe the story of the things that happened in the past.

HOW FOSSILS FORM

Fossils form in different ways, and can be classed on how much of the original creature is left.

A. Organisms preserved in their entirety. These are very rare and include things like insects entombed in amber.

B. The hard parts of living things preserved unaltered, such as sharks' teeth in Tertiary sediments.

C. Only some of the original substance of the living thing left. Leaves can break down leaving a thin film of the original carbon in the shape of the leaf. This produces coal.

D. Petrified living things: the original organic substance which is replaced molecule by molecule to produce a fossil with the original structure but made entirely of mineral. Petrified wood is a result of this.

E. Mould. This is a hole left in the rock when all the original organic material has decayed away. A special kind of mould forms from the hollow between the shells of a bivalve seashell.

F. Cast. When a mould (see E) is filled by minerals deposited by ground water, the result is a lump in the shape of the original body, but does not have the internal structure. A cast can form in the space between the valves of seashells, showing us the shape of the interior of the shells.

G. Trace fossils. Sometimes nothing of the original organism is left – just its burrows or the marks that it made, showing us how it lived but not what it looked like. Dinosaur footprints are important trace fossils.

Petrified wood

THE USES OF FOSSILS

Apart from showing us the history of life on Earth, fossils can be used for a number of purposes.

A. Index fossils. Some animals or plants only existed for a short period of time. When we find the fossils of such animals in a rock, we know that the rock must have formed during that time. By observing the presence of fossils with overlapping time periods, we can date that rock even more precisely.

B. Facies fossil. Some animals or plants can only live under specific environmental conditions. When we find fossils of these creatures, we can deduce that the rocks in which they are entombed must have formed under these conditions. Index fossils are important to oil geologists who are looking for rocks that formed under the right conditions to produce oil.

BEFORE FOSSILIZATION

All sorts of things happen to an organism before it is fossilized.

• It can be eaten, or partially eaten, by other animals.

• It may rot away.

• It may break down under the influence of the weather.

This is why it is very unlikely for any individual organism to be preserved as a fossil. All this activity is known as taphonomy.

DURING FOSSILIZATION

- For an organism to become a fossil it must be buried rapidly in sediment. This will ensure that none of the taphonomic effects will take place.

- This is why we mostly find fossils of animals that live in the water, where sediment is accumulating, and why fossils of land-living animals are very rare.

- The remains are then affected in various ways, producing the different fossil types on page 12.

- The process that takes place as the sediment becomes sedimentary rock, is known as diagenesis.

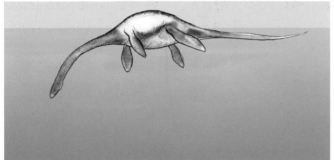

FOSSIL ASSEMBLAGES

Fossils are not usually found individually. Many are found together as groups called assemblages.

A. Life assemblage. This occurs when the fossils reflect how the animals and plants lived. In a life assemblage the bivalve molluscs are still joined together and attached animals like sea lilies are in their growth positions. It is as if the whole community had just dropped dead on the spot. This is very valuable in working out how the animals lived.

B. Death assemblage. This occurs when the dead animals and plants are washed about by currents and end up all jumbled together. We can identify a death assemblage by the fact that bivalve shells are broken apart and maybe aligned in the direction of the current; delicate skeletons are disarticulated and scattered; and fossils from nearby environments are mixed up with them.

Death assemblage (left) and life assemblage (right).

AFTER FOSSILIZATION

Once a fossil is formed, it lies deep beneath the surface of the Earth, maybe several kilometres down.
If we are ever to find it, it must be brought to the surface. This usually happens if the sedimentary rocks that contain it are caught up in mountain-building processes through the actions of plate tectonics. The rocks may be

Finding dino fossils.

twisted and crushed up so that they end up as mountains well above sea level. The wind and the rain then act on them to break them down, forming new material for clastic sedimentary rocks.

The fossil-bearing beds may then be exposed to our view.

See pages 8-9 for more information on plate tectonics.

PRECAMBRIAN

There is a long sequence of opening titles and scene-setting before we get to the exciting bit of our film. However, this part of the film is all important. During much of Precambrian time, life was developing from mere molecules that had the ability to reproduce, like viruses, through the formation of single cells, like bacteria, to creatures that were made up of many cells. Some of these creatures were the precursors of today's life forms.

PRECAMBRIAN (2500-543 MYA) TIMELINE

Precambrain	Proterozoic	Neoproterozoic
		Mesoproterozoic
		Palaeoproterozoic
	Archaean	
	Hadean	

EVIDENCE OF LIFE TIMELINE

3.5 billion years
Signs of where microbes may have eaten into newly erupted basalt flows on the sea bed.

600 million years
The earliest known multicelled organisms, like sea anemones come from the Mackenzie Mountains in Canada.

0.8 billion years
Evidence of life can be found in the Bitter Springs Chert in Australia.

2 billion years
Gunflint chert microfossils show evidence of life in Canada.

3.465 billion years
Possible lifeforms in microfossils in the Apex Chert in Australia.

3.5 billion years
Microfossils in Swaziland show signs of life.

(The chert in which most of these are found is a glassy sedimentary rock made of silica)

VENDIAN PERIOD

The very end of the Neoproterozoic is known as the Vendian. Fossils of multi-celled animals are known from this period, but nothing with a hard shell.

Many scientists would like include the Vendian in the Palaeozoic rather than the Precambrian.

PRECAMBRIAN WORLD

Since the Precambrian covers over 85 percent of the Earth's history, it is difficult to make general statements about it. The world in Precambrian times had more ocean, and the continents were still small.

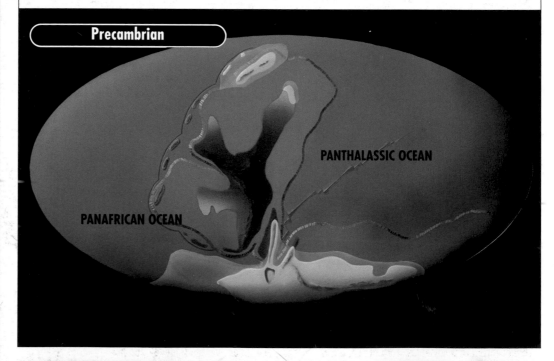

Precambrian

PANTHALASSIC OCEAN

PANAFRICAN OCEAN

STROMATOLITES

The earliest good fossils discovered are of stromatolites. These occur when microscopic filaments of algae or bacteria attract particles of sediment and form a mat. Other mats build up on this to form a dome-like structure.

The oldest stromatolites are 3.5 billion years old.

Nowadays we find them in the Red Sea and around Australia in sheltered salty bays where there are no other living things to disturb their growth.

A fossilized stromatolite

Modern stromatolites in Australia.

It is possible that between 750 and 580 million years ago the Earth was entirely frozen. As this would have been just before many-celled animals appeared, it is possible that the return to equable climates after such a drastic event spurred the burst in evolution.

Evidence
- Glaciated rocks in Australia and other continents from that time, formed at sea level near the equator.

- Limestones formed at the time show evidence that they would have formed in very cold water.

- Lack of oxygen in the atmosphere is shown by the minerals formed at the time. This would come about if cold conditions killed off nearly all life.

What the Earth may have looked like 750-580 million years ago.

ANIMALS OF THE VENDIAN

The first living things were merely molecules that could reproduce themselves from the chemicals around them. Eventually they became single-celled organisms, firstly with simple prokaryotic cells and then with more complex eukaryotic cells. The latter eventually developed into multi-celled types, the cells forming tissues that built up into individual organs. Amongst the earliest multi-celled organisms were strange soft-bodied things from the Vendian period of Australia and of England. These include *Spriggina* that resembled a segmented worm, and *Charnodiscus*, a feather-like animal similar to the modern sea-pen.

Spriggina

Charnodiscus

EARLY PALAEOZOIC TIMELINE

543-417 MYA

Early Palaeozoic		
	Silurian	Pridoli
		Ludlow
		Wenlock
		Llandovery
	Ordovician	Bala
		Dyfed
		Canadian
	Cambrian	Merioneth
		St David's
		Caerfai

PALAEOZOIC ERA

The Palaeozoic era is made up of six periods. The first three make up the early Palaeozoic period and the other three are the Devonian, Carboniferous and the Permian.

Permian 290-248

Carboniferous 354-290

Devonian 417-354

Early Palaeozoic 543-417

LAND ANIMALS

Although we say that there were no land animals in the early Paleozoic, we know of some strange trace fossils from Canada, from the Cambrian period. They were made by a soft-bodied animal. The flat-bodied animal hauled itself along the damp sand of the Cambrian shoreline. The animal had flaps on either side of its body and dug those into the sand to pull itself forward, creating tracks that look like motorcycle tracks.

uring this time, our film of the Earth's history is starting to get exciting. However, nearly all the action takes place at the bottom of the sea. All sorts of hard-shelled animals have evolved by this time and all the main groups that exist today had come into being. By the end of this section, life was beginning to quit the waters and come out on to land.

SILURIAN PERIOD 443-417

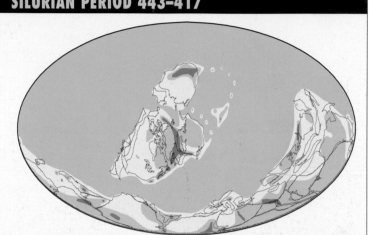

Meaning: From Silures – an old Welsh tribe.
Continents were continuing to move together. The edges of the continents were flooded, giving large areas of shallow sea over continental shelves. Many reefs and shallow-water organisms existed at that time. The first land-living plants appeared.

ORDOVICIAN PERIOD 490-443

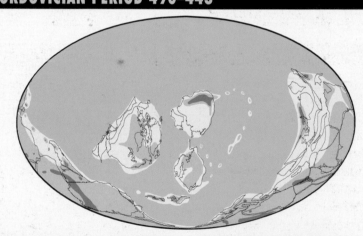

Meaning: From Ordovices – an old Welsh tribe.
In the Ordovician period the northern landmasses were beginning to move towards one another. An ice age took place at the boundary with the Silurian, 450 to 440 million years ago.

CAMBRIAN 543-490

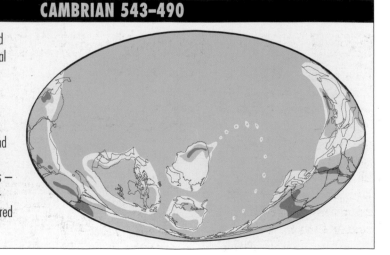

Meaning: From Cambria – an old name for Wales, where the original work was done on the lower Paleozoic rocks.
In the early Palaeozoic all of the southern continents – South America, Africa, India, Australia and Antarctica – were part of a single landmass. The northern continents – North America, Europe and Asia – were individual landmasses scattered over the ocean.

THE BURGESS SHALE

The most spectacular set of Cambrian fossils lies in the Burgess Shale in Canada. These consist of all kinds of animals, most of which don't seem to fit into any established classification. It is as if nature were trying out every shape imaginable as soon as hard animal parts had evolved, just to see what would work and what would not.

Burgess shale animals

Marella — like a trilobite with long horns on its head.

Nectocaris — like a shrimp's body with an eel's tail.

Opabinia — like a worm with a trunk and many pairs of paddles.

Wiwaxia — like a slug covered in chain mail.

Hallucigenia — a worm-like body with tentacles along one side and stilts along the other.

Anomalocaris — a big swimming predator that probably hunted all these.

See page 55 for more information on Charles Doolittle Walcott who discovered the Burgess Shale.

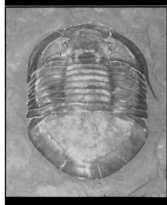

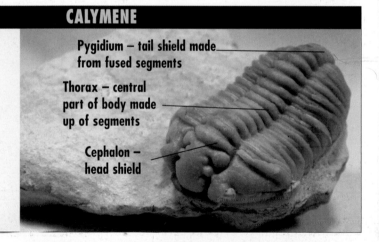

The Burgess Shale in Canada today.

CALYMENE

Time: Silurian
Size: About 3 cm (1 $\frac{3}{16}$ in)
Diet: Organic particles from sea bed
Habitat: Shallow seas
Information: *Calymene* was a typical trilobite — one of the most abundant of the sea-living arthropods in the early Paleozoic.

Pygidium – tail shield made from fused segments

Thorax – central part of body made up of segments

Cephalon – head shield

DIPLOGRAPTUS

Time: Silurian
Size: 5 cm (2 in) each branch
Diet: Suspended organic particles
Habitat: Open water
Information: *Diplograptus* was a common graptolite — a floating colonial organism. It consisted of two rows of living creatures back to back, and several hanging suspended from a gas float.

Other graptolites include *Monograptus*, with a single row of individuals, and *Didymograptus*, with two rows arranged in a wishbone shape. These are all valuable index fossils for the early Paleozoic.

See pages 12-13 for more information on index fossils.

Isotelus

Period: Silurian

Diet: Buried organic matter

Habitat: In sandy sea bottoms

Information: Spade-shaped trilobite, smooth surface, adapted for burrowing.

Eodiscus

Period: Cambrian

Diet: Floating organic matter

Habitat: Open water

Information: Tiny early trilobite, free swimming, only two segments in the thorax, cephalon the same size as pygidium.

Olenellus

Period: Cambrian

Diet: Organic detritus

Habitat: Shallow sea bed

Information: An early trilobite, tiny pygidium, spines on the segments.

Cryptolithus

Period: Ordovician

Diet: Floating organic matter

Habitat: Open water

Information: Free-swimming trilobite, huge cephalon with long spines at the rear, small thorax and pygidium.

Devonian	Famennian Frasnian	D3
	Givetian Eifelian	D2
	Emsian Pragian Lochkovian	D1

DEVONIAN

During this period, animals began to leave the water and live on land. In the previous Silurian period, the first land plants appeared. The first land-living animals would be insects, living in this vegetation. Then came the vertebrates – transitional forms between fish and amphibians. They would have been attracted by the new food supplies on land, or may have taken refuge from the ferocious fish and sea scorpions that lived in the water.

PLANTS

The earliest land plants consisted of nothing but a stem, supporting a reproductive body. By the end of the Devonian there were forests of horsetails and ferns.

THE AGE OF FISHES

Although fish had already evolved, they did not become important until the Devonian – in fact it is known as the Age of Fishes.

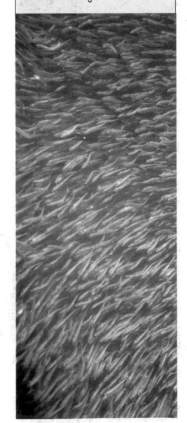

THE WORLD IN THE DEVONIAN

The Devonian period is named after the county of Devon in the United Kingdom, where rocks of the era are well represented.

During this time, the continents were beginning to move together. The ancestors of Europe and North America collided forming a single continent – the Old Red Sandstone continent – with an enormous mountain range crumpled up between the two. The remains of this mountain range are found in the Scottish and Norwegian Highlands and part of the Appalachians in North America.

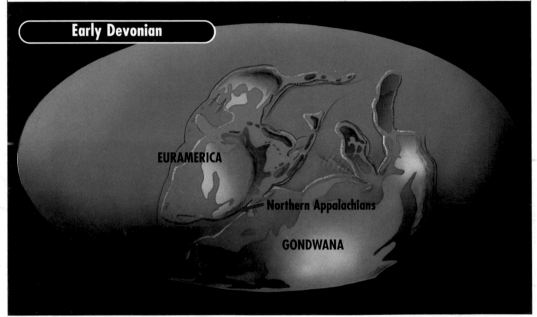

Early Devonian

EURAMERICA

Northern Appalachians

GONDWANA

CHANGING ATMOSPHERE

The atmosphere during the early part of Earth's history was a toxic mix of poisonous gases that no animal could breathe. By the Devonian it had changed, with oxygen being added by the action of plant life, both in the water and on land. This made it possible for the land to be colonized.

Atmosphere at the Earth's beginning

Other 3%
N 12%
H_2 10%
CO_2 75%

Precambrian atmosphere

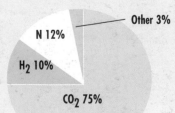

CO_2 10%
Other 15%
N 75%

Devonian atmosphere

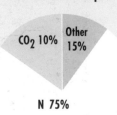

O_2 25%
N 75%

OLD RED SANDSTONE

This type of rock is typical of Devonian times. Formed from river gravels and desert sandstones, it turned red through oxidisation of the iron in it by exposure to air.

See pages 10-11 for more information on different rock types.

CEPHALASPIS

Meaning: Head spike
Time: Late Silurian – Early Devonian
Size: 50 cm (19 ft 5 in)
Diet: Organic detritus
Habitat: Shallow water
Information: This early fish had no jaws, just a sucker to allow it to scoop up food from the sea bed.

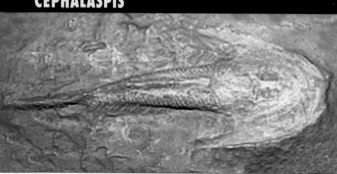

EUSTHENOPTERON

Meaning: Properly strong fin
Time: Late Devonian
Size: 1 m (3 ft 3 in)
Diet: Other fish
Habitat: Shorelines
Information: A fish that shows adaptations to life on land. The fins were in pairs and had bones and muscles allowing for movement over dry surfaces. A lung enabled it to breathe air.

ICHTHYOSTEGA

Meaning: Fish-roof
Time: Late Devonian
Size: 1 m (3 ft 3 in)
Diet: Fish and insects
Habitat: Shorelines
Information: One of the earliest of amphibians. *Ichthyostega* still had a fish's skull and a fish's tail. Its hind limbs had eight toes – the standard five-toed pattern had not yet evolved.

ANIMAL PROFILES

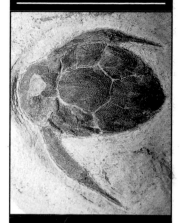

Bothriolepis
Time: Early Devonian
Diet: Organic detritus
Habitat: Lakes
Information: One of the armoured fish – a group common in Devonian times. It had armoured jointed front fins.

Dunkleosteus
Time: Late Devonian
Diet: Other fish
Habitat: Open ocean
Information: A giant form of the armoured fish – one of the biggest of the time.

Climatius
Time: Early Devonian
Diet: Other fish
Habitat: River mouths
Information: One of the so-called "spiny sharks" with heavy scales and a double row of fins along its belly.

Cladoselache
Time: Late Devonian
Diet: Other fish
Habitat: Open ocean
Information: An early shark, looking very similar to modern forms – the shape of sharks has not changed much over the years.

CARBONIFEROUS

CARBONIFEROUS TIMELINE
354-290 MYA

Carboniferous	**Pennsylvanian**	Gzelian
		Kasimovian
		Moscovian
		Bashkirian
	Mississippian	Serpukhovian
		Visean
		Tournaisian

By the Carboniferous period, life on the land had become fully established. It is the time of coal forests inhabited by gigantic insects and other arthropods, and by the first reptiles. The period came to an end with an ice age that affected most of the southern hemisphere.

ONE PERIOD OR TWO?

In Europe, the Carboniferous is regarded as a single period. In America it is split in two.

Pennsylvanian — 323-290 mya. Equivalent to the Late Carboniferous or the Upper Carboniferous.

Mississippian — 354-323 mya. Equivalent to the Early Carboniferous or the Lower Carboniferous.

Upper and Lower Carboniferous are terms used when we are talking about the rock sequences or the fossils formed. Early and Late Carboniferous are terms used when we are talking about the events of the time, such as the evolution of reptiles.

THE WORLD IN THE CARBONIFEROUS

The period is named after the element carbon, which was abundant at this time.

During the Carboniferous, newly-thrown-up mountain ranges were being quickly eroded and the debris spread out into broad river deltas. These were clothed in thick forests that eventually formed the coal seams of the period.

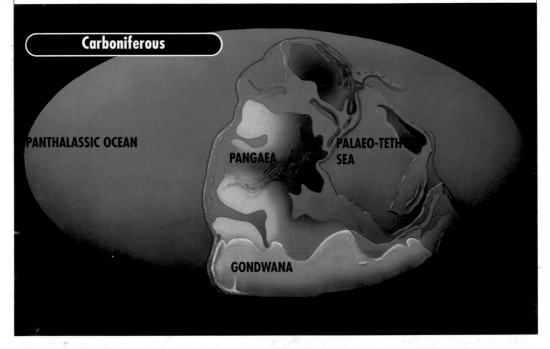

Carboniferous

PANTHALASSIC OCEAN

PANGAEA

PALAEO-TETHYS SEA

GONDWANA

FORMATION OF COAL

1. The plant layers soaked up water and were pressed together, forming a brown, spongy material called peat.

3. More heat and pressure, at greater depths, turned the lignite into a soft, black coal called bituminous coal.

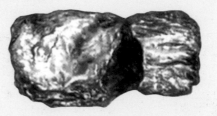

2. More sediment layers formed on top of the peat, burying it deeper and deeper. The greater pressure and heat turned the peat into a brown coal called lignite.

4. This turned finally into a harder, shiny black coal called anthracite.

COAL FOREST PLANTS

Lepidodendron – a club moss growing to 30 metres (98 ft 4 in) high, consisting of a straight trunk that branched dichotomously (into two equal branches, then into two again and so on) with long strap-shaped leaves. Trunk covered in diamond-shaped leaf scars.

Sigillaria – a club moss similar to *Lepidodendron* but with leaf scars arranged in parallel rows.

Calamites – horsetails as big as Christmas trees. Growing as reed beds in shallow water.

Cordaites – a primitive relative of the conifers, growing on slightly drier ground. Various ferns forming undergrowth and creeping up the trunks.

EOGYRINUS

Meaning: Early twister
Time: Late Carboniferous
Size: 5 m (16 ft 4 in)
Diet: Fish and other amphibians
Habitat: Coal swamps

Information: One of the big amphibians of the period, it cruised the shallow waters of the coal swamp like an alligator, looking for other animals to eat. *Eogyrinus* could spend some time on land but it needed to return to the water to breed.

MEGANEURA

Meaning: Big nerves
Time: Late Carboniferous
Size: 1.5 m (4 ft 9 in) wingspan
Diet: Not known
Information: Like a dragonfly, but the size of a magpie, *Meganeura* was typical of the very large arthropods that existed in the coal forests. Others included centipedes that were as big as pythons.

WESTLOTHIANA

Meaning: From the county of Westlothian in Scotland
Time: Early Carboniferous
Size: 20 cm (7 $^7/_8$ in)
Diet: Small insects

Information: *Westlothiana* is either the earliest reptile known, or it is something intermediate between the amphibians and the reptiles. Certainly it was the precursor of the land-living animals to come.

ANIMAL PROFILES

Hylonomus
Time: Late Carboniferous

Diet: Insects

Habitat: In the trunks of coal forest trees

Information: An early reptile, looking very much like a modern lizard.

Diplovertebron
Time: Late Carboniferous

Diet: Insects and other amphibians

Habitat: Coal swamps

Information: A big amphibian.

Crassigyrinus
Time: Early Carboniferous

Diet: Fish and other amphibians

Habitat: Coal swamps

Information: Amphibian with tiny limbs, a big head and a tapering body – totally aquatic.

Ophiderpeton
Time: Late Carboniferous

Diet: Small invertebrates

Habitat: Moist leaf litter

Information: An amphibian that had totally lost its legs and lived like an earthworm in the leaf litter.

Arthroplura
Time: Late Carboniferous

Diet: Rotting vegetable matter

Habitat: Coal swamps

Information: A gigantic millipede, 1.8 metres (5 ft 9 in) long.

PERMIAN

Permian	Zechstein	Changxingian
		Longtanian
		Capitanian
		Wordian
		Ufimian
	Rotliegendes	Kungurian
		Artinskian
		Sakmarian
		Asselian

At the beginning of the Permian period, the southern hemisphere was still in the grip of the ice age that started at the end of the Carboniferous. Once this had cleared up, the continents were gripped in a desert period – forming the "New Red Sandstone". The end of the Permian shows a severe bout of volcanic activity, mostly in Siberia.

DESERT FEATURES

Desert features seen in Permian rocks:
- Dune bedding
- Red sandstones showing dry oxidation environments
- Beds of coarse pebbles that have been shaped by the wind

THE WORLD IN THE PERMIAN

This period is named after the Perm region in Russia, where the rocks dating from this time are well exposed. In the Permian, nearly all the continents had accumulated into a single landmass. The mountains of Devonian and Carboniferous times were being eroded into hills, and there was less erosion forming river deltas. The coal forests dried up and were replaced by deserts.

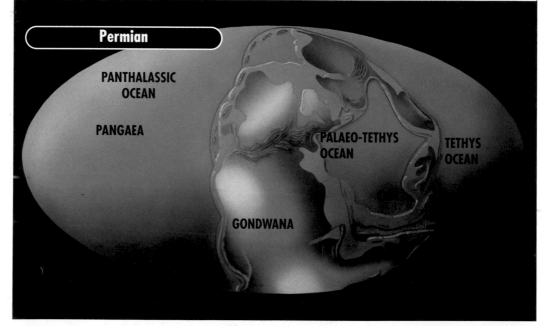

Permian

PANTHALASSIC OCEAN

PANGAEA

PALAEO-TETHYS OCEAN

TETHYS OCEAN

GONDWANA

REEFS

The kinds of animals that lived in the seas in the earlier part of our film made their last appearance in Permian times. In the region of Texas, there were thick reefs. Modern reefs are made of corals. Permian reefs were made of:
- Sponges
- Algae
- Bivalves
- Crinoids (sea lilies)
- Brachiopods (animal with two shells but unrelated to bivalves)

The Permian reefs of Texas contain the state's oil reserves.

MESOSAURUS

Meaning: Middle lizard
Time: Early Permian
Size: 1 m (3 ft 3 in)
Diet: Small swimming animals
Information: The age of reptiles had well and truly arrived, with swimming and flying forms as well as land-living types. Fossils of *Mesosaurus*, a freshwater swimmer, have been found in South Africa and Brazil, showing that this area was all one continent at that time.

PAREIASAURUS

Meaning: Side-by-side lizard
Time: Middle Permian
Size: 2.5 m (8 ft 2 in)
Diet: Plants
Information: Plant-eating vertebrates appeared at this time. Big-bodied types like *Pareiasaurus* fed on the ferns and conifers of the desert oases.

DIMETRODON

Meaning: Two sizes of tooth
Time: Early Permian
Size: 3 m (9 ft 8 in)
Diet: Other reptiles
Information: An important group of reptiles were the mammal-like reptiles that eventually gave rise to the mammals. *Dimetrodon* was an early example. It had a sail on its back to help regulate its temperature in the desert heat.

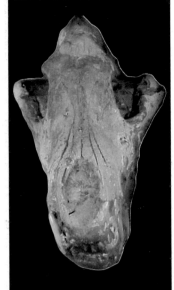

Moschops

Time: Late Permian

Diet: Plants

Habitat: Deserts

Information: A big plant-eating mammal-like reptile.

Eryops

Time: Late Permian

Diet: Fish and other amphibians

Habitat: Desert streams

Information: One of the big amphibians that still existed at this time.

Seymouria

Time: Early Permian

Diet: Insects and small vertebrates

Habitat: Deserts

Information: Had features that were transitional between amphibians and reptiles.

Lycaenops

Time: Late Permian

Diet: Other reptiles

Habitat: Deserts

Information: A mammal-like reptile that looked like a mammal.

Triassic	Rhaetian Norian Carnian	Tr₃
	Ladinian Anisian	Tr₂
	Spathian Nammalian Griesbachian	Scythian, Tr1

MESOZOIC ERA

The Triassic period is the first of the three periods that make up the Mesozoic era.
The other two are the Jurassic and the Cretaceous.

Cretaceous 144-65

Jurassic 206-144

Triassic 248-206

GLOSSOPTERIS

A new kind of plant – *Glossopteris* (a kind of fern that reproduced by seed) – became very common. Its fossils are found throughout the southern continents.

TRIASSIC

After the Permian scene closes, our film begins to change dramatically. The boundary between the Permian and the Triassic coincides with the greatest mass-extinction in Earth's history, with 95 per cent of species wiped out. Scientists do not know whether the volcanic activity in Siberia had anything to do with it, but following the event, whole new groups of animals spread over the land and through the sea.

THE WORLD IN THE TRIASSIC

All the continents had now come together to form one great supercontinent we call Pangaea.

All the oceans were likewise combined into one superocean called Panthalassa. The New Red Sandstone conditions continued,

with arid deserts in the hinterland of the continent. Land life was only possible around the moist edges.

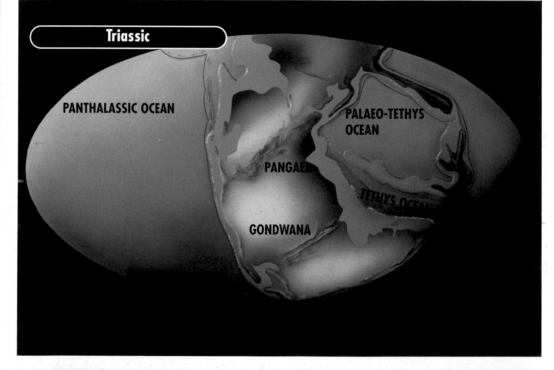

Triassic

PANTHALASSIC OCEAN

PALAEO-TETHYS OCEAN

PANGAEA

TETHYS OCEAN

GONDWANA

MEANING OF THE NAME

Trias – three. Refers to the three sequences of rock in Germany where the period was first identified. These are:
Keuper – desert sandstones and marls.
Muschelkalk – (mussel chalk) limestone marking a marine phase.
Bunter – desert sandstones.
Classification still used, even though in most of Europe the Muschelkalk is absent.

Muschelkalk

NEW PLANT LIFE

Differences between the plants of the Permian and Triassic are as follows.

Trees
Permian – giant club mosses and cordaites, just like the Carboniferous coal forests.

Triassic – primitive conifers like monkey puzzle trees.

Medium-sized plants
Permian – giant horsetails, tree ferns.

Triassic – cycad-like plants, tree ferns.

Small plants
Permian – seed ferns and horsetails.

Triassic – conventional ferns and horsetails.

REASONS FOR THE MASS EXTINCTION

No-one is sure. There are several theories.

1. The change to the atmosphere caused by the eruptions in Siberia.

2. Climate fluctuation caused by the coming together of all the continents.

3. Meteorite impact. Chemical evidence has been found in Australia and Antarctica, but it is not strong.

4. Change in the saltiness of the ocean.

TRIASSIC CLIMATES

Because all the land was in a single supercontinent, the climates were extreme. They could be divided into a number of belts.
1. Year round dry climate.

2. Sharply season rainfall near the coasts.
3. High latitude regions of cool rains.
The interior of Pangaea was stiflingly hot during the Triassic, with little rain falling. Warm

temperatures extended down to the Earth's poles. Scientists think that this was one of the hottest periods of the planet's history, with gobal warming occurring towards the end of the Triassic.

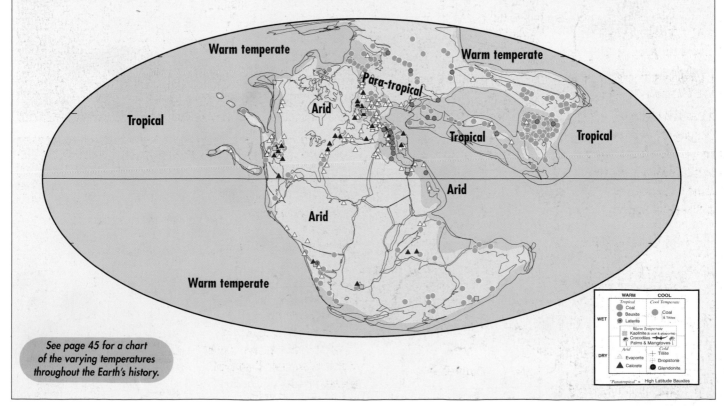

See page 45 for a chart of the varying temperatures throughout the Earth's history.

TRIASSIC LIFE

There is a significant change of cast in the Triassic sequence of our film. Gone are the myriad sea creatures of the Palaeozoic era, to be replaced by totally new types of water-living animals. The changing plant life on the land feeds a changing animal life. The land animals continue to develop and expand, some developing flying and swimming lifestyles, and the first mammals and dinosaurs appear.

HARD-SHELLED EGG – THE KEY TO LAND-LIVING

There were still plenty of big amphibians on Earth at this time, but it is the beginning of the Age of Reptiles.

- Reptiles have a hard-shelled egg – amphibians lay soft eggs that must be nurtured in the water.
- Reptiles hatch fully formed from the egg – amphibians go through a larval "tadpole" stage, usually in the water.
- Reptiles have a tough waterproof skin that can stand up to dry conditions – amphibians have a soft skin covered in mucus that must be kept moist.

CHANGING PLANTS, CHANGING ANIMALS

The evolving plant life encouraged an evolving animal life as well. The plant-eating mammal-like reptiles declined as the seed-ferns died out.
A new line of plant-eating mammal-like reptile evolved as the conventional ferns took over.

Mammals and dinosaurs evolved, and the conifers established themselves at the end of the period.

Dinosaurs evolved to eat the conifers.

New reptiles, called rhynchosaurs evolved to eat the conventional ferns.

Mammal-like reptiles ate seed-ferns.

FOOTPRINTS

Evidence of reptile existence comes from the many footprints found in Triassic sandstones.

Famous localities include – Dinosaur State Park in Connecticut, Moab, Utah (both in the United States) and Dumfriesshire, Scotland. Scotland.

See pages 12-13 for more information on fossils.

WHAT MAKES A DINOSAUR?

There are several features that define a dinosaur and make it different from all other reptiles.
These are –

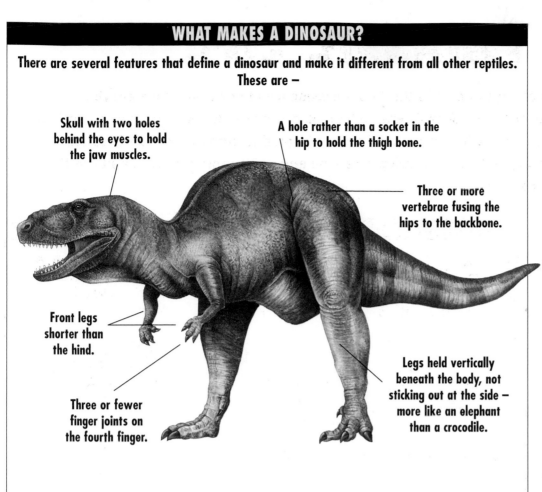

Skull with two holes
behind the eyes to hold
the jaw muscles.

A hole rather than a socket in the
hip to hold the thigh bone.

Three or more
vertebrae fusing the
hips to the backbone.

Front legs
shorter than
the hind.

Three or fewer
finger joints on
the fourth finger.

Legs held vertically
beneath the body, not
sticking out at the side –
more like an elephant
than a crocodile.

Nothosaurus

Time: Late Triassic

Diet: Fish

Habitat: Shallow seas

Information: Swimming
reptile that hunted fish from
land.

Mixosaurus

Time: Late Triassic

Diet: Fish

Habitat: Shallow seas

Information: One of the
earliest ichthyosaurs, the
fish-shaped swimming
reptiles of the Mesozoic.

Hyperodapedon

Time: Middle Triassic

Diet: Ferns

Habitat: Desert oases

Information: A rhynchosaur
– one of the important plant-
eaters before the dinosaurs.

Tanystropheus

Time: Late Triassic

Diet: Fish

Habitat: Shallow seas

Information: A strange long-
necked shore-living animal.

Erythrosuchus

Time: Early Triassic

Diet: Other animals

Habitat: Deserts

Information: An early
crocodile relative that was
the fiercest hunter before
the dinosaurs.

EORAPTOR

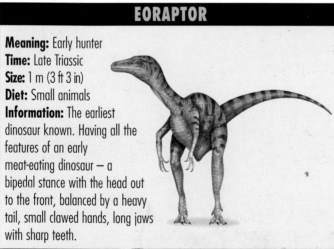

Meaning: Early hunter
Time: Late Triassic
Size: 1 m (3 ft 3 in)
Diet: Small animals
Information: The earliest
dinosaur known. Having all the
features of an early
meat-eating dinosaur – a
bipedal stance with the head out
to the front, balanced by a heavy
tail, small clawed hands, long jaws
with sharp teeth.

THECODONTOSAURUS

Meaning:
Socket-
toothed lizard
Time: Late Triassic
Size: 1 m (3 ft 3 in)
Diet: Plants
Information: One of
the first of the plant-eating
dinosaurs. *Thecodontosaurus* had a
bigger body than a meat-eater, to

hold a more complex digestive
system and a small head and a long
neck to reach its food.

EUDIMORPHODON

Meaning: True two shapes
of teeth
Time: Late Triassic
Size: 1 m (3 ft 3 in) wingspan
Diet: Fish
Information: One of the earliest
pterosaurs – a group of flying
reptiles, related to dinosaurs, that
were the lords of the skies in the
Mesozoic era. *Eudimorphodon's*
wings were formed by wing
membranes supported by a
long finger.

	Malm	Tithonian
		Kimmeridgian
		Oxfordian
Jurassic	Dogger	Callovian
		Bathonian
		Bajocian
		Aalenian
	Lias	Toarcian
		Pliensbachian
		Sinemurian
		Hettangian

JURASSIC

This is one of the most famous sequences of our film, when the real stars appear on screen. Although the dinosaurs appeared in the previous Triassic period, it was really in the Jurassic that they took over and became the most successful creatures on the Earth at that time. The deserts were waning now, because the supercontinent of Pangaea was splitting up and spreading arms of the ocean and shallow seas across the landmass.

MASS EXTINCTIONS

There were three mass-extinction events that took place at this time.

1. At the boundary between the Triassic and Jurassic. This killed off the last of the mammal-like reptiles.

2. During the Pleinsbachian stage of the lower Jurassic. This affected much of the dinosaur fauna.

3. At the very end of the Jurassic period. This had a greater effect on sea animals than land animals.

None of these was particularly large.

THE WORLD IN THE JURASSIC

The beginning the Jurassic period was still a time of deserts. However, as the age progressed, rift valleys appeared across Pangaea and the supercontinent began to break up.

The most famous rift valley is the zig-zag rift that began to split the Americas from Europe and Africa. This would eventually form the Atlantic Ocean.

As North America begins to move westwards, the Rocky Mountains begin to crumple up before it.

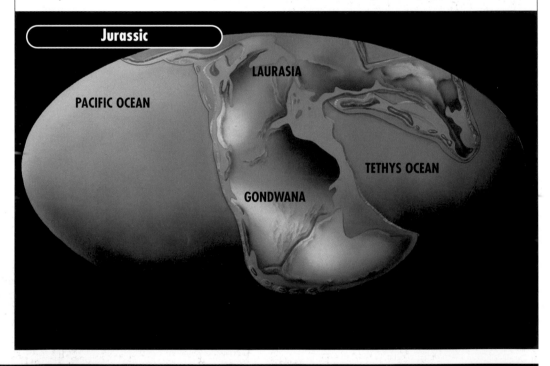

Jurassic

PACIFIC OCEAN

LAURASIA

TETHYS OCEAN

GONDWANA

MEANING OF THE NAME

The Jurassic is named after the Jura Mountains, that offshoot of the Alps between Switzerland and France, where von Humboldt first studied the limestones in 1795.

TYPICAL JURASSIC ROCKS

Oolitic limestone — Chemical sedimentary rock made up of fine pellets of calcite. This rock is good as a building material.

Lias — A series of interbedded limestone and deep water shale from the earliest part of the period. It was laid down as deep water muds, and the limestone separated out as it solidified.

See pages 10-11 for more information on different rock types.

TWO JURASSIC ROCK SEQUENCES

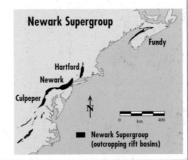

The Newark Supergroup — A series of (mostly) sandstones, laid down in rift valleys along the east coast of North America, showing where Pangaea was beginning to break apart.

Newark Supergroup

Fundy

Hartford

Newark

Culpeper

N

0 km 400

■ Newark Supergroup (outcropping rift basins)

The Morrison Formation — A sequence of river sandstones, shales, conglomerates and evaporates laid down on an arid plain, criss-crossed by rivers in the Late Jurassic of the American mid-west.

ECONOMIC IMPORTANCE

The rocks that formed in the Jurassic period are extremely important in today's world as building materials and fuel.

- The oilfields of the North Sea are formed in Jurassic rocks.
- Much of London is built from late Jurassic Portland limestone.

ANIMAL PROFILES

Rhomaleosaurus

Time: Early Jurassic

Diet: Fish

Habitat: Shallow seas

Information: A plesiosaur with a big head – almost an intermediate form between plesiosaurs (long-necked) and pliosaurs (short-necked).

Ichthyosaurus

Time: Early Jurassic

Diet: Fish

Habitat: Open ocean

Info: A medium-sized ichthyosaur which resembled a modern-day shark. It had a slim, pointed snout and foreflippers twice as large as its hind flippers.

INDEX FOSSILS

The different marine beds of the Jurassic are dated using species of ammonites — relatives of squids and cuttlefish that left fossils of coiled shells.

Each species only existed for a few million years and so the rocks in which they were found can be closely dated. Each species was quite widespread throughout the ocean, so their fossils are common in different parts of the world.

JURASSIC LIFE

I t is because the majority of fossils are found in marine deposits, that the fossils of sea-living animals are more abundant than those of land-living ones. This does not mean that life was more abundant in the water than on land during the Jurassic, but nevertheless the sea life was very important at that time. The spreading seas gave rise to broad continental shelves where sediment built up and trapped the fossils of the sea life of the time.

THE LIFE ON A CONTINENTAL SHELF

The animal life inshore was different from that in the open water, which again was different from that of the deep sea bed. Many species have been preserved as fossils in marine limestones and shales.

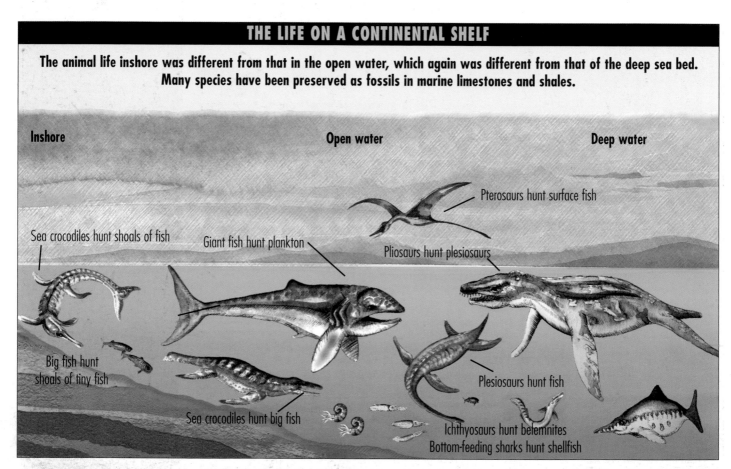

Inshore

Open water

Deep water

Pterosaurs hunt surface fish

Sea crocodiles hunt shoals of fish

Giant fish hunt plankton

Pliosaurs hunt plesiosaurs

Big fish hunt shoals of tiny fish

Sea crocodiles hunt big fish

Plesiosaurs hunt fish

Ichthyosaurs hunt belemnites
Bottom-feeding sharks hunt shellfish

CRYPTOCLIDUS

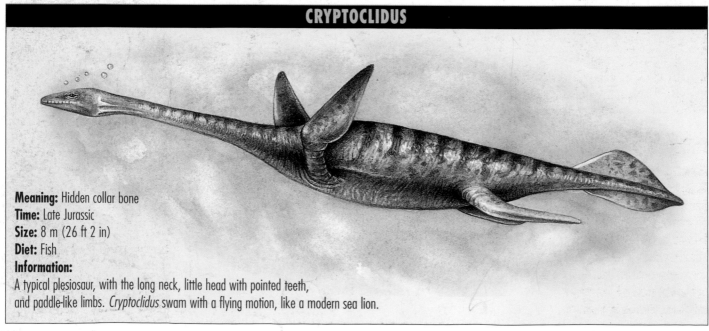

Meaning: Hidden collar bone
Time: Late Jurassic
Size: 8 m (26 ft 2 in)
Diet: Fish
Information:
A typical plesiosaur, with the long neck, little head with pointed teeth, and paddle-like limbs. *Cryptoclidus* swam with a flying motion, like a modern sea lion.

THE FOSSILS OF THE LAGOONS

Along the northern shore of the Tethys Sea – the arm of the ocean that separated the north and south parts of Pangaea – shallow lagoons formed behind reefs built by sponges and corals.

The bottom of the water was toxic, and it killed and preserved many swimming and flying creatures. These formed minutely-detailed fossils in very fine limestone.

See pages 12-13 for more information on fossils.

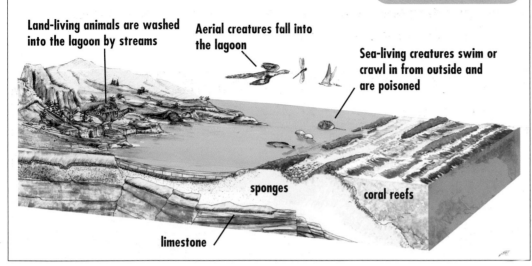

Land-living animals are washed into the lagoon by streams

Aerial creatures fall into the lagoon

Sea-living creatures swim or crawl in from outside and are poisoned

sponges

coral reefs

limestone

ANIMAL PROFILES

Archaeopteryx

Time: Late Jurassic

Diet: Insects

Habitat: Trees

Information: The first bird, but retaining many dinosaur features showing that it was closely related to dinosaurs.

Ophthalmosaurus

Time: Late Jurassic

Diet: Fish

Habitat: Shallow seas

Information: A typical ichthyosaur, having developed the well-known fish shape.

Metriorhynchus

Time: Late Jurassic

Diet: Fish

Habitat: Shallow seas

Information: One of the marine crocodiles, with a fish-like tail and paddle limbs.

Leedsihcthys

Time: Late Jurassic

Diet: Plankton and tiny fish

Habitat: Open seas

Information: One of the biggest fish that ever lived, but feeding on small creatures, like the modern whale shark does.

LIOPLEURODON

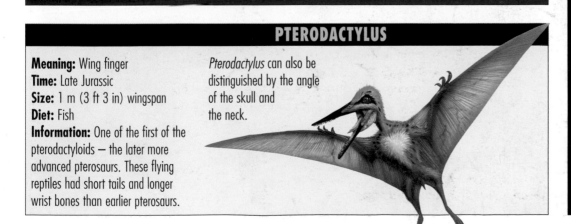

Meaning: Smooth-sided tooth
Time: Late Jurassic
Size: 12 m (39 ft 4 in)
Diet: Fish and plesiosaurs
Information: *Liopleurodon* was one of the big whale-like pliosaurs. Unlike their relatives the plesiosaurs, these had short necks and massive heads. They probably lived a bit like modern sperm whales, hunting big animals.

PTERODACTYLUS

Meaning: Wing finger
Time: Late Jurassic
Size: 1 m (3 ft 3 in) wingspan
Diet: Fish
Information: One of the first of the pterodactyloids — the later more advanced pterosaurs. These flying reptiles had short tails and longer wrist bones than earlier pterosaurs.

Pterodactylus can also be distinguished by the angle of the skull and the neck.

JURASSIC DINOSAURS

The most spectacular animals of Jurassic times were undoubtedly the dinosaurs. They ranged from small fox-sized animals to things that were bigger than modern whales, and they lived on all the continents of the world. Scientists can make out different families of dinosaurs, each with their own lifestyles and habits.

DINOSAUR TYPES

Saurischians (Lizard hips)
These dinosaurs were distinguished by their hips. The three main bones of the hips radiated away from the hole where the leg was attached, as they do in modern lizards. They are divided into several main groups.

Ornithischians (Bird hips)
In this group of dinosaurs, the pubis bone in the hip is swept back along the ischium bone, making room for a big gut which was necessary because these were all plant-eating dinosaurs. They had a bone in the front of the jaw that the saurischians lacked. Several groups are recognized.

Ornithopods (Bird feet). The two-footed plant-eaters, although the biggest ones spent most of their time on all fours.

Theropods (Beast footed) The meat-eaters, walking on their hind legs, with small arms and the big teeth held out to the front.

Therizinosaurs (Scythe claws) These seem to have been plant-eaters but were closely related to the theropods. They were mostly Cretaceous and their hips were more like those of the ornithischians.

Marginocephalians The dinosaurs with armoured heads. Mostly Cretaceous and divided into the boneheads and the horned dinosaurs with the shields around their necks.

Prosauropods (Before the sauropods) The earliest plant-eaters, with long necks and small heads.

Thyreophorans The dinosaurs with armour plates. Further divided into the plated stegosaurs (mostly Jurassic) and the armoured ankylosaurs (mostly Cretaceous).

Sauropods (Lizard feet) The big plant-eating dinosaurs with the massive bodies and the heavy legs, with the very long necks and tails.

A DINOSAUR LANDSCAPE

The most famous dinosaur skeletons were found in the Morrison Formation in western North America.
In the Jurassic period, this area was a broad dry plain between the newly-formed Rocky Mountains and a shallow sea that spread across the centre of the continent. The plain was crossed by many rivers, and it was on the forested river banks that most dinosaurs lived.

See page 29 for more information on the Morrison Formation.

ANIMAL PROFILES

Compsognathus
Time: Late Jurassic
Diet: Lizards
Habitat: Island beaches
Information: A theropod, the smallest dinosaur discovered so far.

Ceratosaurus
Time: Late Jurassic
Diet: Other dinosaurs
Habitat: Open plains
Information: A theropod which was armed with a horn on the snout.

Apatosaurus
Time: Late Jurassic
Diet: Plants
Habitat: Open plains
Information: A sauropod very similar to *Diplodocus*, but shorter and more heavily built.

Megalosaurus
Time: Middle Jurassic
Diet: Other dinosaurs
Habitat: Wooded islands
Information: A theropod, the first dinosaur to be discovered.

Kentrosaurus
Time: Late Jurassic
Diet: Plants
Habitat: Open plains
Information: A thyreophoran, a stegosaur with very narrow plates and many spines.

Brachiosaurus
Time: Late Jurassic
Diet: Tall trees
Habitat: Open plains
Info: A sauropod that went for height rather than length.

STEGOSAURUS

Time: Late Jurassic
Size: 8 m (26 ft 2 in)
Diet: Plants
Information: The plates on the back of *Stegosaurus* were either for protection or they were used as a heat control device. *Stegosaurus'* brain is the smallest relative to the size of the animal for any known dinosaur.

DIPLODOCUS

Time: Late Jurassic
Size: 30 m (98 ft 4 in)
Diet: Plants
Information: *Diplodocus* was a typical sauropod. It was balanced neatly at the hips so it could raise itself up so that its lightweight head and neck could reach into trees. *Diplodocus* used its tail as a defensive whip.

CRETACEOUS TIMELINE

144-65 MYA

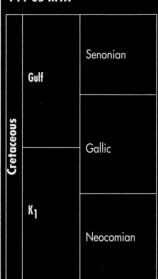

Cretaceous	Gulf	Senonian
		Gallic
	K₁	
		Neocomian

As the Mesozoic continues so the cast of amazing dinosaurs changes again. During the Cretaceous period, the continents moved away from each other and the dinosaurs diversified. The period was brought to a shuddering end by a sudden event that destroys the dinosaurs. The age of reptiles was finished.

THE WORLD IN THE CRETACEOUS

What was left of Pangaea was continuing to pull itself apart. Some of the continents were now in the shapes that we would recognize today.

Much of the southern landmass was still present as a supercontinent throughout the Cretaceous. This comprised what are now South America, Africa, India, Australia and Antarctica. We give this supercontinent the name Gondwana. Now Gondwana was splitting up, with only Australia and Antarctica still joined.

DIVERSE DINOSAURS

There were more dinosaurs around in Cretaceous times than there were previously. This is because all the different isolated continents had different types of dinosaurs evolving on them.

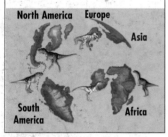

North America   Europe   Asia
South America   Africa

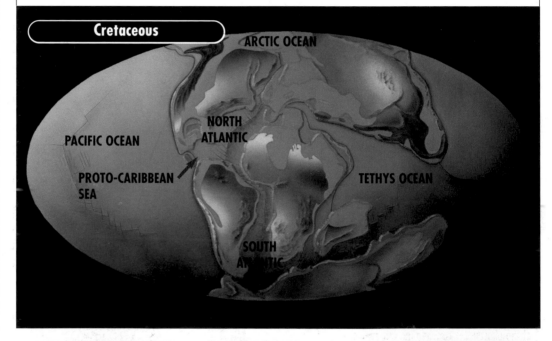

Cretaceous

ARCTIC OCEAN

NORTH ATLANTIC

PACIFIC OCEAN

PROTO-CARIBBEAN SEA

TETHYS OCEAN

SOUTH ATLANTIC

MEANING OF THE NAME

Creta is the Latin name for chalk, and vast deposits of this very fine limestone were laid down on the shallow sea shelves at that time – particularly in southern England, northern France and Kansas in the United States.

See pages 10-11 for more information on different rock types.

TYLOSAURUS

Meaning: Swollen lizard
Time: Late Cretaceous
Size: 10 m (32 ft 8 in)
Diet: Ammonites and other sea animals
Information: A typical big mosasaur. Closely related to modern monitor lizards but with paddle-shaped limbs and a flattened tail. *Tylosaurus* and its relatives would have pursued the same prey and had the same lifestyle as the ichthyosaurs of the preceding Jurassic period.

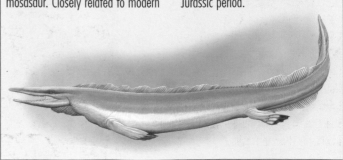

ANIMALS OF AIR AND SEA

The shallow seas that spread everywhere at the end of the period were full of different types of sea animals. The ichthyosaurs were gone, but were replaced by a different group of sea reptiles, the mosasaurs. The pterosaurs continued to rule the skies but the birds were present as well.

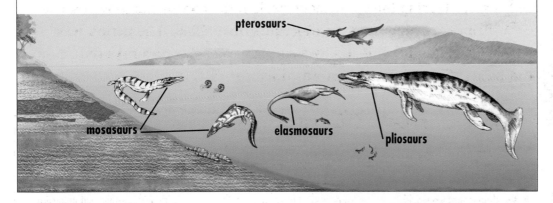

pterosaurs

mosasaurs

elasmosaurs

pliosaurs

Deinosuchus
Time: Late Cretaceous
Diet: Dinosaurs
Habitat: Swamps
Information: The biggest crocodile so far known.

Archelon
Time: Late Cretaceous
Diet: Jellyfish
Habitat: Open ocean
Information: Perhaps the biggest turtle that ever existed.

Pleurosaurus
Time: Early Cretaceous
Diet: Fish
Habitat: Open ocean
Information: Little eel-like swimming reptile related to the modern tuatara.

Pteranodon
Time: Late Cretaceous
Diet: Fish
Habitat: Open ocean
Information: Big toothless fishing pterosaur

Tapejara
Time: Late Cretaceous
Diet: Fruit
Habitat: Forests
Information: Pterosaur with the most flamboyant crest.

Pterodaustro
Time: Late Cretaceous
Diet: Fine crustaceans
Habitat: Inland lakes
Information: A pterosaur with jaws like sieves, like a flamingo.

ELASMOSAURUS

Meaning: Long lizard
Time: Late Cretaceous
Size: 15 m (49 ft 2 in)
Diet: Fish
Information: *Elasmosaurus* had the longest neck of all the plesiosaurs, comprising 71 vertebrae and taking up more than half the length of the whole animal. It swallowed stones to aid digestion and to adjust its balance while swimming.

KRONOSAURUS

Meaning: Lizard of Kronos – a Greek giant
Time: Early Cretaceous
Size: 10 m (32 ft 8 in)
Diet: Ammonites and other sea animals
Information: *Kronosaurus* was the biggest of the pliosaurs – certainly the one with the biggest head, 2.7 metres (8 ft 9 in) long. A creature's skull was found in Australia but none of the rest of the body has been unearthed yet.

ARAMBOURGIANIA

Meaning: Named after Camille Arambourg, who first described it in the 1950s
Time: Late Cretaceous
Size: 12 m (39 ft 4 in) wingspan
Diet: Fish probably
Information: Scientists keep finding bigger and bigger pterosaur bones and announcing that this must have been the biggest animal that could possibly fly. The current record holder is *Arambourgiania*.

CRETACEOUS LIFE

During the Cretaceous period, the main groups of dinosaurs, the saurischians and the ornithischians, continued to be strong, but they all developed into different forms on the different continents. Of the saurischians, the plant-eating sauropods were not as important as they had been. The big meat-eating theropods can be regarded as the villains of our film drama, while the smaller types took a lesser role, but their characters developed in another direction – scientists think that they survived as the modern birds.

Alamosaurus

Time: Late Cretaceous

Diet: Trees

Habitat: Woodland

Information: The last sauropod of North America.

Sauroposeidon

Time: Early Cretaceous

Diet: Trees

Habitat: Woodland

Information: One of the last and biggest of the brachiosaurs.

Argentinasaurus

Time: Late Cretaceous

Diet: Trees

Habitat: Woodland

Information: A titanosaur. The heaviest dinosaur yet discovered.

Baryonyx

Time: Early Cretaceous

Diet: Fish

Habitat: River banks

Information: A crocodile-snouted fishing theropod.

Ornithomimus

Time: Late Cretaceous

Diet: Omnivorous

Habitat: Open country

Information: Ostrich-like and fleet of foot.

Protoceratops

Time: Late Cretaceous

Diet: Desert vegetation

Habitat: Desert and scrubland

Information: An early horned-dinosaur.

SALTASAURUS

Meaning: Lizard from Salta
Time: Late Cretaceous
Size: 12 m (39 ft 4 in)
Diet: Trees

Information: By the end of the Cretaceous the only important sauropods belonged to the titanosaur group. They mainly lived in the southern continents and many of them had backs covered in armour.

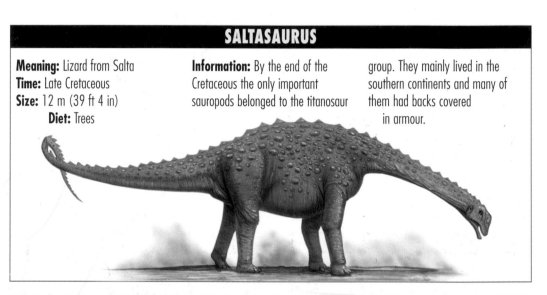

CAUDIPTERYX

Meaning: Wing tail
Time: Early Cretaceous
Size: 70 cm (2 ft 3in)
Diet: Insects

Information: One of the small theropods that show distinctive bird features. It was very lightly built and had feathers on the wings and the tail. However the wings were too small to allow it to fly. Here it is shown in the bottom, right of the picture.

VELOCIRAPTOR

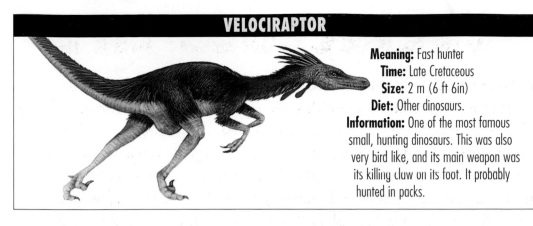

Meaning: Fast hunter
Time: Late Cretaceous
Size: 2 m (6 ft 6in)
Diet: Other dinosaurs.
Information: One of the most famous small, hunting dinosaurs. This was also very bird like, and its main weapon was its killing claw on its foot. It probably hunted in packs.

TYRANNOSAURUS

Meaning: Tyrant lizard
Time: Late Cretaceous
Size: 10 m (32 ft 8 in)
Diet: Other dinosaurs
Information: Once regarded as the biggest of the meat-eating dinosaurs, it is certainly still the most widely known, with its huge head and its steak-knife teeth as big as bananas. The tiny arms are still a bit of a mystery.

THERIZINOSAURUS

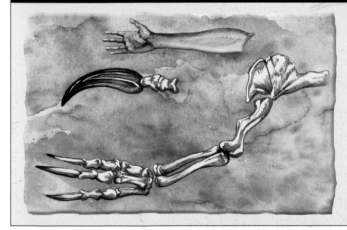

Meaning: Scythe lizard
Time: Late Cretaceous
Size: 8 m (26 ft 2 in)
Diet: Plants
Information: *Therizinosaurus* was the biggest of the therizinosaurs. It had big arms with the most enormous claws of any dinosaur. Claw bones measuring 70 cm (2 ft 3 in) have been unearthed. They may have been used for pulling down branches to reach the leaves on which it fed.

CARNOTAURUS

Meaning: Flesh-eating bull
Time: Late Cretaceous
Size: 10 m (32 ft 8 in)
Diet: Other dinosaurs
Information: While the tyrannosaurs were the biggest meat-eaters of north America, another group, the abelisaurs were the largest carnivores in the southern continents. *Carnotaurus*, with its bull-like horns, was a typical abelisaur.

ANIMAL PROFILES

Oviraptor
Time: Late Cretaceous
Diet: Not known, maybe eggs
Habitat: Open country
Information: Small theropod with a heavy bird-like bill.

Sinosauropteryx
Time: Early Cretaceous
Diet: Insects and small animals
Habitat: Lakesides
Information: A typical tiny theropod, but covered in feathers.

Spinosaurus
Time: Late Cretaceous
Diet: Other dinosaurs
Habitat: Open country
Information: Carried a spectacular fin on its back.

Masiakasaurus
Time: Late Cretaceous
Diet: Fish
Habitat: Riversides
Information: A snaggle-toothed fish-hunting abelisaur.

Troodon
Time: Late Cretaceous
Diet: Smaller animals
Habitat: Woodlands
Information: A big-eyed fast hunter, probably the most intelligent of dinosaurs.

CRETACEOUS PLANT-EATERS

Stygimoloch

Time: Late Cretaceous

Diet: Low vegetation

Habitat: Open woodland

Information: Bone-headed dinosaur with a spectacular array of horns.

Ouranosaurus

Time: Early Cretaceous

Diet: Trees

Habitat: Open woodland

Information: A sail-backed relative of *Iguanodon*.

Corythosaurus

Time: Late Cretaceous

Diet: Trees

Habitat: Woodland

Information: Duckbill with a semicircular crest.

Tsintaosaurus

Time: Early Cretaceous

Diet: Trees

Habitat: Woodland

Information: Duckbill with a single spike for a crest.

Anatotitan

Time: Late Cretaceous

Diet: Trees

Habitat: Woodland

Information: One of the duckbills that had no crest.

Polacanthus

Time: Early Cretaceous

Diet: Low vegetation

Habitat: Open woodland

Information: An early ankylosaur.

With the wide range of landscapes and plant types that existed in the Cretaceous, a wide range of plant-eating dinosaurs, mostly ornithischians, evolved to make the best use of it. When we think of dinosaurs, we tend to think of saurischians. However, it was the ornithischian types which flourished at this time, with many more species than the saurischians.

NEW PLANTS

Flowering plants producing seeds appeared in early Cretaceous times and spread rapidly at the end of the period. Possible reasons include:

Magnolia

Oak

Willow

Birch

• Grazing by dinosaurs put such a pressure on plant life that they evolved quick-growing seeds to repair the damage.

• Increasing temperatures towards the end of the period encouraged tougher reproductive structures like seeds.

By the end of the period there were many familiar plants, the landscape began to look like it does today. However, grass had yet to evolve.

No actual fossil flowers have been found, but scientists can work out what species might have flourished by looking at fossils of seeds, leaves, wood and pollen grains.

VARIED HABITATS

Different plants live in **different places**. It is possible that the new plants flourished on the well-watered lowlands, while the old plants — the cycads and the old-style conifers — continued in the hills. The typical Cretaceous plant-eaters, evolved to tackle the new food, would have lived on the lowlands, while the older types, like the waning sauropods, would have remained in the hills.

***Saltasaurus* was a sauropod.**

See page 36 for more information on Saltasaurus.

EUOPLOCEPHALUS

Meaning: Well-armoured head
Time: Late Cretaceous
Size: 6 m (19ft 7 in)
Diet: Low-growing vegetation.
Information: The ankylosaurs took over from the stegosaurs as the armour-carrying dinosaurs of the Cretaceous period. There were three families — the primitive polacanthids, the ankylosaurids such as *Euoplocephalus* with clubs on the ends of their tails, and the nodosaurids that had spikes on their shoulders instead.

IGUANODON

Meaning: Iguana tooth
Time: Early Cretaceous
Size: 10 m (32 ft 8 in)
Diet: Trees and low-growing vegetation.
Information: *Iguanodon* was one of the first dinosaurs to be discovered.

A complex chewing action with jawbones that moved in relation to each other; batteries of grinding teeth; and cheeks to hold the food, meant that this dinosaur could tackle all kinds of plant food.

PARASAUROLOPHUS

Meaning: Like a lizard crest
Time: Late Cretaceous
Size: 10 m (32 ft 8 in)
Diet: Trees and low-growing vegetation.
Information: *Parasaurolophus* was one of the duckbilled dinosaurs, which evolved from something like *Iguanodon*. This group spread to become the most important plant-eating animals of the northern hemisphere at the end of the Cretaceous. Many had strange crests on their heads.

TRICERATOPS

Meaning: Three-horned head
Time: Late Cretaceous
Size: 8 m (26 ft 2 in)
Diet: Bushes and low-growing vegetation.
Information: *Triceratops* was part of a group of horned dinosaurs called ceratopsians. This group evolved from small, rabbit-sized animals at the beginning of the Cretaceous to rhinoceros-sized beasts with heavy shields on their heads by the end of the period.

ANIMAL PROFILES

Archaeoceratops
Time: Early Cretaceous
Diet: Low vegetation
Habitat: Desert
Information: Small ancestral horned dinosaur.

Edmontonia
Time: Late Cretaceous
Diet: Low vegetation
Habitat: Open woodland
Information: A typical nodosaurid ankylosaur.

Struthiosaurus
Time: Late Cretaceous
Diet: Low vegetation
Habitat: Islands
Information: A dwarf nodosaurid ankylosaur.

Ankylosaurus
Time: Late Cretaceous
Diet: Low vegetation
Habitat: Open woodland
Information: The biggest of the ankylosaurid ankylosaurs.

Styracosaurus
Time: Late Cretaceous
Diet: Low vegetation
Habitat: Open plains
Information: Horned dinosaur with a single horn and spikes around the neck.

Psittacosaurus
Time: Early Cretaceous
Diet: Plants and small animals
Habitat: Desert-like scrubland
Information: *Psittacosaurus* was around for 40 million years: the longest-lived type of dinosaur.

THE GREAT EXTIN- TION

At the end of the Cretaceous period (and the end of the Mesozoic era) there was a great extinction. It was not the only mass-extinction to have taken place in the Earth's history, or even the greatest. However, it does seem to be the one that has caught everybody's imagination. Not only did it wipe out the dinosaurs, but it also took the pterosaurs and the great sea reptiles of the time.

DISEASES

As the continents continued to move, and the sea levels fluctuated, land bridges began to open up between one continent and another. Animals of one continent would have been free to migrate to another and mingle with the animals there. These newcomers would have brought diseases to which they were immune, but to which the local population would be vulnerable. Exchange of diseases like this would have weakened the populations so much that extinction would have followed.

Evidence
The mass extinction in the oceans seems to have taken place anything up to half a million years before that on land, suggesting that something immediate and catastrophic like a meteorite impact was not to blame.
The largest animals of the world were affected, something that we see today if plagues spread through natural populations.

WHAT CAUSED THE GREAT EXTINCTION?

Scientists are still not sure what led to the catastrophic loss of life at the end of the Cretaceous, but there are several serious suggestions:

Meteorite or comet strike

Volcanic activity

Changing climates

Diseases

Many palaeontologists believe a combination of all of these factors wiped out the dinosaurs.

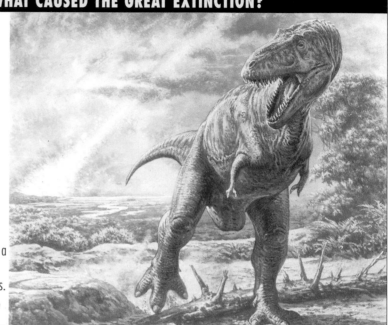

METEORITE OR COMET STRIKE

The most popular theory is that a body from space struck the Earth 65 million years ago. This would have had several effects.

- Shock waves would have killed everything in the vicinity.

- Seismic sea waves (tsunamis) would have flooded all the lowlands.

- Hot molten debris would have caused widespread wildfires.

- Clouds of dust would have cut off the sunshine, causing short-term global cooling.

This disrupted atmosphere would have produced a long-term greenhouse effect.

Evidence
- A buried structure looking like a meteorite crater of the right size and age has been found in Yucatan in Mexico.

- Sedimentary rocks have been discovered in Texas that look like tsunami deposits.

- Deposits of the element iridium

— only found abundantly in meteorites or beneath the Earth's crust, have been detected in a layer all over the world.

- Deposits of quartz crystals have been unearthed that show signs of being deformed by a heavy impact.

CHANGING CLIMATES

The dinosaurs and the other big animals may have become so well adapted to the equable climates of the Mesozoic Era that they did not have the capability to cope with any dramatic change.

Evidence
- The end of the Cretaceous period shows signs of increasing temperatures.
- Dinosaur eggshells of the time show signs of weakening — evidence of heat stress.
- There have been observations of changing sea levels of the time which would influence climates.
- Replacement of tropical forest with temperate woodland took place, indicating a sudden cooling after the increasing temperatures.

A COMBINATION OF ALL OF THESE

There seems to be evidence that the dinosaurs were fading in the last few million years of the Cretaceous.
If this is so, then a meteorite impact could have just finished them off.

The Yucatan impact site at the time was exactly at the other side of the world from the area of the Deccan Trapps. Perhaps the two are linked. The impact in Yucatan could have set up vibrations through the Earth that focused on the other side and generated the volcanic activity.

Perhaps the meteor broke in two, one part hitting Yucatan and the other hitting India 12 hours later, inducing the vulcanism. Disease and plague would inevitably spread through populations weakened by natural disaster.

WINNERS AND LOSERS

The exinction event wiped out significant percentages of species of most groups.

From this chart we see that mammals and birds were heavily affected. They were, however, small and adaptable, and able to recover quickly.

Throughout the Mesozoic, mammals had been small and shrew-like — totally insignificant. This was about to change.

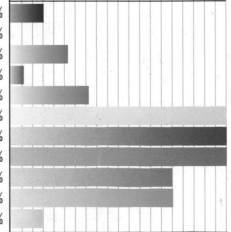

Fish lost	15%
Amphibians	0%
Tortoises and turtles	27%
Lizards and snakes	6%
Crocodiles	36%
Dinosaurs	100%
Pterosaurus	100%
Plesiosaurs	100%
Birds	75%
Marsupial mammals	75%
Placental mammals	14%

VOLCANIC ACTIVITY

Widespread volcanic activity would put so much debris and gas into the atmosphere that the climates would change — in the same way as would be caused by a meteorite impact. The deposits of iridium could have been brought to the Earth's surface by volcanoes.

Evidence
Half of the sub-continent of India is made up of basaltic lava flows (called the Deccan Trapps) that erupted at the end of the Cretaceous period, 65 million years ago, which could have wiped out the entire dinosaur population.

REPENOMAMUS

Meaning: Fearsome mammal
Time: Early Cretaceous
Size: 1 m (3 ft 3 in)
Diet: Dinosaurs!
Information: Found in lake deposits in China, this dog-sized mammal had the bones of small dinosaurs in its stomach.

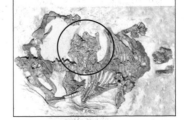

After the Great Extinction, the set of our film looks rather the same as it did before – equable climates and thick forest over most of the land. The cast seems to have changed, though. With the big reptiles gone, the Age of Mammals was about to begin. This age included the eventual evolution of the first hominid.

TERTIARY TIMELINE

65-1.8 MYA

Tertiary	Neogene	Pliocene
		Miocene
	Palaeogene	Oligocene
		Eocene
		Palaeocene

ANIMAL PROFILES

Ambulocetus

Time: Eocene

Diet: Meat

Habitat: Shallow seas

Information: The earliest-known whale. Swam rather like a sea lion.

Uintatherium

Time: Eocene

Diet: Leaves

Habitat: Forests

Information: One of the various big rhinoceros-like mammals.

Leptictidium

Time: Eocene

Diet: Insects

Habitat: Shallow seas

Information: Swift, long-legged little insectivore.

Indricotherium

Time: Oligocene

Diet: Trees

Habitat: Woodland

Information: A gigantic rhinoceros. The biggest land animal known.

THE WORLD IN THE EARLY TERTIARY

By this period, the continents of the world had moved into an almost recognizable form. The major differences in the image below are that Australia had only just broken away from Antarctica and was beginning its long trek northwards towards the equator, and India was still an island in its dash across the Indian Ocean from Africa.

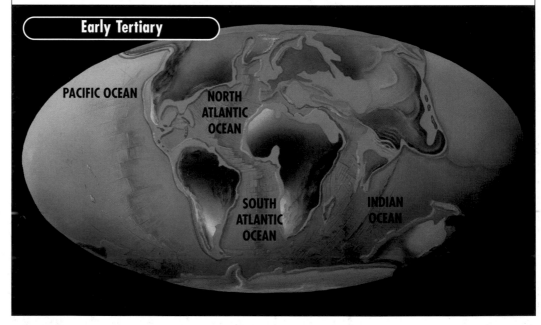

Early Tertiary

PACIFIC OCEAN

NORTH ATLANTIC OCEAN

SOUTH ATLANTIC OCEAN

INDIAN OCEAN

PLANT AND ANIMAL LIFE

The plant life is similar to that of the late Cretaceous, with thick forests of modern type plants.

There is still not much in the way of grass. The animal life is totally different as the mammals have taken over. Like at the beginning of the Cambrian, it is as if all sorts of new shapes are being tried out just to see what works. Mammals live:

- On the land, replacing the dinosaurs.
- In the sea, replacing the plesiosaurs and mosasaurs.
- In the air, replacing the pterosaurs.
- Birds are also important. At the beginning of the period there are flightless birds that are like their dinosaur ancestors, and these are the main predators of the time.

MEANING OF THE NAME

The term "tertiary" comes from an old Victorian dating system —

Primary — what we would call the Precambrian and the Palaeozoic.

Secondary — what we would call the Mesozoic.

Tertiary — from the end of the dinosaurs to the Ice Age.

Quaternary — the Ice Age and the present day.

The last two terms are still used. The Tertiary is divided into the early Tertiary — the Palaeogene — and the late Tertiary — the Neogene.

MAMMAL NAMES

Many mammal names end with "-therium", an old Greek name for "beast", just like many dinosaur names end with "-saurus", an old Greek name for "lizard".

BRONTOTHERIUM

Meaning: Thunder beast
Time: Oligocene
Size: 2 m (6 ft 6in) tall
Diet: Low vegetation
Information: Many of the larger mammals developed into rhinoceros shapes with big bodies to digest plants and horns on the head for defence. *Brontotherium* was one of these types of mammals.

HYRACOTHERIUM

Meaning: Hyrax beast
Time: Eocene
Size: 50 cm (1 ft 6 in) long
Diet: Leaves
Information: *Hyracotherium* was the earliest member of the horse family. It was only the size of a hare, and had teeth for chewing leaves from bushes, not grass from the ground.

DIATRYMA

Time: Palaeocene to Eocene
Size: 2 m (6 ft 6 in) tall
Diet: Mammals
Information: With the lack of carnivores around, some birds become the main hunters, taking on the appearance of their dinosaur ancestors. *Diatryma* is an example of such a bird.

OXYAENA

Name: Oxyaena
Meaning: Sharp claw
Time: Eocene
Size: 50 cm (1 ft 6 in) long
Diet: Small animals
Information: The meat-eating mammals became established with the creodonts, which were similar in appearance but unrelated to modern carnivores.

Icaronycteris
Time: Eocene
Diet: Insects
Habitat: Trees
Information: The earliest bats were almost identical to modern forms.

Plesiadapis
Time: Palaeocene
Diet: Leaves
Habitat: Trees
Information: An early member of the primate group, like a lemur.

Hypsodus
Time: Eocene
Diet: Seeds and fruits
Habitat: Treetops
Information: A short-legged squirrel-like climber.

Chriacus
Time: Eocene
Diet: Fruits, insects and small animals
Habitat: Undergrowth
Information: A generalized mammal with forelimbs adapted for digging.

Buxolestes
Time: Eocene
Diet: Shellfish
Habitat: Lakes
Information: An otter-like swimming mammal with strong teeth.

Presbyornis
Time: Eocene
Diet: Small things in the mud
Habitat: Lakes
Info: A long-legged duck.

ANIMAL PROFILES

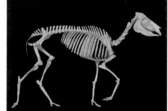

Neohipparion

Time: Miocene

Diet: Grass

Habitat: Grasslands

Information: The horses are now plains animals, with grass-eating teeth.

Alticamelus

Time: Miocene

Diet: Leaves

Habitat: Woods

Information: Camel with a long giraffe-like neck.

Megantereon

Time: Miocene

Diet: Big animals

Habitat: Grasslands

Information: The true cats were beginning to evolve, including some with big teeth.

Paleoparadoxia

Time: Miocene

Diet: Seaweed or shellfish

Habitat: Shorelines

Information: A massive amphibious mammal that may have lived like a walrus.

Cranioceras

Time: Miocene

Diet: Leaves

Habitat: Subtropical woodland

Information: A deer-like hoofed mammal. A third horn grew upward and back from the rear of the skull and was used for fighting.

D uring this period, the Earth's appearance began to change dramatically. The forests died away and grasslands spread everywhere. This was caused by a general cooling of the climate. The spreads of open plains encouraged the evolution of a new kind of animal – long-legged for running over wide expanses, and with specialized digestive systems for breaking down the tough new grass.

THE WORLD IN THE LATE TERTIARY

The late Tertiary world has taken on a very familiar appearance. The main differences between it and the present day is the fact that North America is still separated from South America, and a large area of sea and island chains lies over southern Europe. This sea area is the result of the continent of Africa moving towards Europe and throwing up the Alps from the intervening marine sediments as it goes.

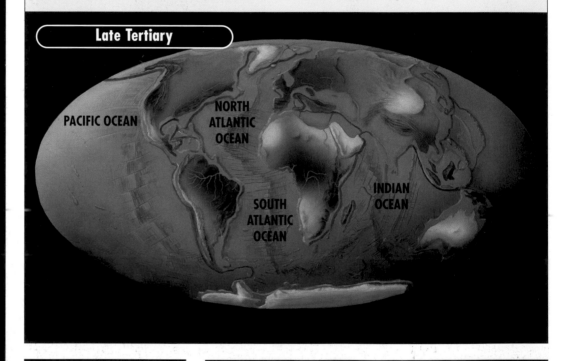

Late Tertiary

PACIFIC OCEAN

NORTH ATLANTIC OCEAN

SOUTH ATLANTIC OCEAN

INDIAN OCEAN

PHORUSRHACOS

Meaning: Terror bird
Time: Miocene
Size: 2.5 m (8 ft 2 in) tall
Diet: Large animals
Information: South America, still isolated from North America, had all kinds of strange animals that existed nowhere else in the world. *Phorusrhacos* was a fast runner and could outrun most of its prey.

THE COMING OF GRASS

The evolutionary advantage of grass is that the main part of its growing stem lies underground.
The exposed leaves can be eaten by grazing animals or burnt off in fires, but the main part is protected in the soil. This makes it ideal for open habitats in very dry climates.

The tough leaves, full of silica, mean that extra hard teeth and complex digestive systems are needed by any animal that evolves to eat it.

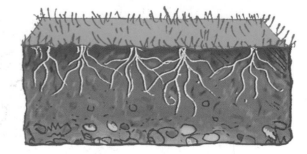

DEINOTHERIUM

Meaning: Terrible beast
Time: Miocene to Pliocene
Size: 2 m (6 ft 6 in) tall
Diet: Ground plants
Information: Many kinds of elephant established themselves at this time. *Deinotherium* had downward-curving tusks on the lower jaw.

SYNTHETOCERAS

Meaning: Fused horn
Time: Miocene
Size: 1.5 m (4 ft 9 in) long
Diet: Grass
Information: Typical grass-eating animals living on plains have long faces, so that their eyes are high up and they can see danger coming from a long way away, and long legs so that they can run away from it. *Synthetoceras* had all of these features.

SIVATHERIUM

Meaning: Beast of Siva
Time: Pliocene
Size: 2 m (6 ft 6 in) long
Diet: Ground plants
Information: The giraffes were more important in Tertiary times than they are now. Many groups thrived between the Miocene and the recent past. All of these groups had bony horns called ossicones. *Sivatherium* was an early example of these early giraffes, with a massive body and a huge set of horns. However, it looked more like a deer than a giraffe.

COOLING CLIMATE

Throughout the history of the Earth we have noted fluctuating atmospheric temperatures, producing changing climates. Towards the end of the Tertiary, there is a distinct cooling off.

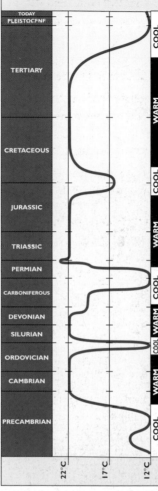

TODAY		COOL
PLEISTOCENE		
TERTIARY		WARM
CRETACEOUS		COOL
JURASSIC		WARM
TRIASSIC		
PERMIAN		COOL
CARBONIFEROUS		
DEVONIAN		WARM
SILURIAN		COOL
ORDOVICIAN		WARM
CAMBRIAN		
PRECAMBRIAN		COOL
22°C	17°C	12°C

ANIMAL PROFILES

Thylacosmilus
Time: Pliocene
Diet: Big animals
Habitat: Grasslands
Information: A South American marsupial that looked like and lived like a sabre-toothed tiger.

Epigaulus
Time: Miocene
Diet: Roots and tubers
Habitat: Grasslands
Information: A burrowing horned rodent.

Dimylus
Time: Miocene
Diet: Insects and small water animals
Habitat: Rivers
Information: A small aquatic insectivore, like a desman.

Daphoneus
Time: Miocene
Diet: Small animals, carrion and plants
Habitat: Plains
Information: A relative of the dog, that lived like a bear.

Eurhinodelphis
Time: Miocene
Diet: Fish
Habitat: Open ocean
Information: A dolphin with a swordfish-like snout.

Platybelodon
Time: Miocene and Pliocene
Diet: Leaves, grasses, bark
Habitat: Grasslands, forests
Information: Elephant with shovel-like tusks.

QUATERNARY

The film of the Earth's history is drawing to a close. The cooling experienced at the end of the late Tertiary becomes extreme, as the world slips into the last ice age. As the ice caps spread outwards from the poles and downwards from the mountain tops, altering the climate throughout the world, the animal life changes to adapt to these harsh new conditions.

THE WORLD IN THE QUATERNARY

The map of the world in the Ice Age shows how much of it was covered in glaciers. Apart from that there seems to be some difference in the coastline, especially around the southern tip of South America and the East Indies. The ice caps have absorbed so much of the ocean's water that the sea level is everywhere very much lower, exposing wide areas of continental shelf where this has been quite shallow.

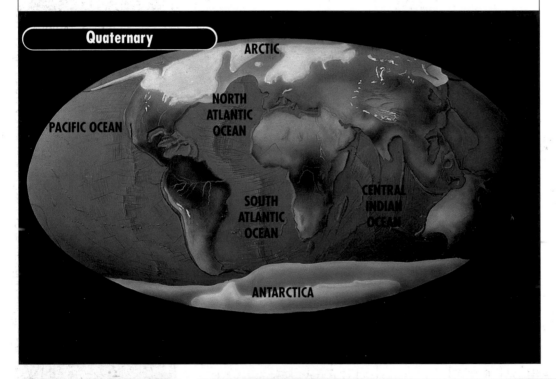

Quaternary

ARCTIC

PACIFIC OCEAN

NORTH ATLANTIC OCEAN

SOUTH ATLANTIC OCEAN

CENTRAL INDIAN OCEAN

ANTARCTICA

CAUSES OF THE ICE AGE

There are several possible events which caused the last ice age:

- Wobble of the Earth's axis.
- Variation in the Earth's orbit, affecting the amount of sunlight received.
- Joining of North and South America closing off the seaway between the warm Pacific and the Atlantic. This made the Atlantic colder and affected the polar ice cap.

MEANING OF THE NAME

The fourth division of geological time, as devised by the Victorians. See page 43.

AGES OF THE QUATERNARY

Most of the period is taken up by the Pleistocene. This is the Ice Age. The rest is the Holocene, or the present day, and this only occupies the last ten thousand years or so.

GLACIAL STAGES

The Ice Age was not a single continuous cold snap. There were glacial periods when the ice was at its most extensive, and interglacials when the climate was warm — often warmer than it is now.

GLACIALS (Europe)

Würm	125,000 to 10,000 years ago
Riss	360,000 to 235,000 years ago
Mindel	7,800,000 to 670,000 years ago
Gunz	1.15 million to 900,000 years ago
Donau	1.6 million to 1.37 million years ago

GLACIALS (North America)

Wisonsinian	30,000 to 8,000 years ago
Illinoian	300,000 to 130,000 years ago
Several ill-defined pre-Illinoian	
	2.5 million to 500,000 years ago

Ocean sediment studies show that there were many fine divisions within these glaciation events.

EVIDENCE OF GLACIATION

Landforms dating from the time
(*Clockwise from top, left*)

- Striations (deep scratches on solid rock surfaces)

- Moraine (heaps of debris carried and deposited by glaciers)

- Kettle holes (lakes formed where an abandoned lump of glacier melted)

- Raised beaches (formed by higher sea level when the local area was pushed down by the weight of the ice cover)

Biological evidence
- Pollen of cold-adapted plants found in lake deposits of the time.

- Skeletons of cold-adapted animals.

Glyptodon
Time: Pleistocene

Diet: Low plants

Habitat: Grassland

Information: A giant armadillo-like animal from South America.

Coelodonta
Time: Pleistocene

Diet: Grass and moss

Habitat: Tundra

Information: The woolly rhinoceros.

Megaceros
Time: Pleistocene

Diet: Grass and moss

Habitat: Tundra

Information: A giant elk with a magnificent spread of horns.

Diprodoton
Time: Pleistocene

Diet: Grass and moss

Habitat: Grassland

Information: Part of the fauna of isolated Australia, like a giant wombat.

Megalania
Time: Pleistocene

Diet: Big animals

Habitat: Desert

Information: A giant monitor lizard – proof that the age of reptiles was not finished!

SMILODON

Meaning: Sabre tooth
Time: Pleistocene
Size: 2 m (6 ft 6 in) long
Diet: Big mammals
Information: The famous sabre-toothed tiger evolved to be able to kill the big plant-eaters of the time.

ELEPHAS PRIMIGENIUS

Time: Pleistocene
Size: 2 m (6 ft 6in) tall
Diet: Ground plants
Information: The woolly mammoth was typical of the big animals of the time. It developed deposits of fat and a shaggy coat to protect against the cold.

MEGATHERIUM

Meaning: Big beast
Time: Pleistocene
Size: 3 m (9ft 8 in) tall
Diet: Trees
Information: Several types of giant ground sloth existed at the time, evolving in South America but spreading to North America as the Central American isthmus was established.

MACRAUCHENIA

Meaning: Big llama
Time: Pleistocene
Size: 2 m (6 ft 6 in) tall
Diet: Ground plants
Information: The isolated South America still provided a home to some strange beasts. *Macrauchenia* was a long-legged long-necked animal with a trunk.

THE FIRST HUMANS

The closing scene of the film is the one that sees the appearance of the first human beings. From our remote ancestors: the unicellular Precambrian organisms, we can trace our ancestry through the fish, the amphibians, the mammal-like reptiles, the primitive shrew-like mammals, the lemur-like early primates, the monkey-like forms, the ape-like forms to a stage where distinctive human features are beginning to appear – upright posture, nimble hands and the ability to make and use tools.

Australopithecus africanus

Time: Pliocene. 3-2.3 million years ago

Diet: Omnivorous

Habitat: Open grassland

Information: The first to be found, in 1924.

Australopithecus anamensis

Time: Pliocene. 4.2-3.9 million years ago

Diet: Omnivorous

Habitat: Open grassland

Information: The earliest-known *Australopithecus* species.

Australopithecus afarensis

Time: Pliocene. 4-2.75 million years ago

Diet: Omnivorous

Habitat: Open grassland

Information: Known as "Lucy". Still with ape-like jaw and fingers.

Australopithecus bahrelghazali

Time: Pliocene

Diet: Omnivorous

Habitat: Open grassland

Information: 3.5-3 million years ago. More modern jaw than *Australopithecus afarensis*.

WHEN AND WHERE DID HUMANS FIRST APPEAR?

From fossils, scientists have discovered that the first human-like mammals lived on the eastern side of Africa at the beginning of the Pleistocene.

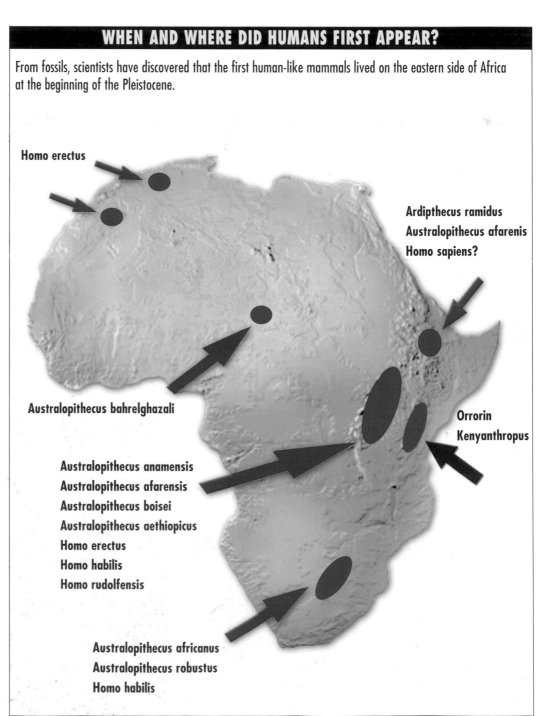

Homo erectus

Ardipthecus ramidus
Australopithecus afarenis
Homo sapiens?

Australopithecus bahrelghazali

Orrorin
Kenyanthropus

Australopithecus anamensis
Australopithecus afarensis
Australopithecus boisei
Australopithecus aethiopicus
Homo erectus
Homo habilis
Homo rudolfensis

Australopithecus africanus
Australopithecus robustus
Homo habilis

WHY DID WE STAND UPRIGHT?

Upright stance probably due to –

- Fewer trees with the onset of the ice age, forcing ape-like animals to live more on the ground.

- Tall grasses forced the need for walking tall, to see over them.

- A vertical animal would be less susceptible to sunburn than one down on all fours.

- Hands that were once used for climbing in branches would now be free for other purposes.

- Brain at the top of a vertical spinal column would have a better chance to enlarge than one at the end of a horizontal one.

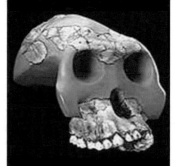

Australopithecus garhi
Time: Pliocene. 2.5 million years ago

Diet: Omnivorous

Habitat: Open grassland

Information: Possibly a tool-user.

Australopithecus aethiopicus
Time: Pliocene. 2.5 million years ago

Diet: Omnivorous – tough, grainy foods

Habitat: Open grassland

Information: This species is known as the "Black Skull" as one fossil absorbed minerals during fossilisation which gave it a black colour.

Australopithecus robustus
Time: Pleistocene. 1.8-1.5 million years ago

Diet: Plants

Habitat: Open grassland

Information: A heavily-built species with muscular jaws and a flat face.

Australopithecus boisei
Time: Pliocene to Pleistocene. 2.3-1.4 million years ago

Diet: Plants

Habitat: Open grassland

Information: Very large jaws and teeth, nicknamed "nutcracker man".

See page 55 for more information on Louis Seymour Bazett Leakey who discovered key species of Australopithecus.

ORRORIN

Meaning: Original man
Time: Miocene. Dating from about 6 million years ago
Size: 1 m (3 ft 3 in) tall
Diet: Omnivorous
Information: The primate that seems to represent the split between the ape lineage and the human lineage.

ARDIPITHECUS

Meaning: Ground ape
Time: Pliocene. 4.4 million years ago
Size: 1 m (3 ft 3 in) tall
Diet: Omnivorous
Information: Better-known than the older *Orrorin* and more widely regarded as the oldest hominid.

KENYANTHROPUS

Meaning: Kenyan ape
Time: Pliocene. 3.5-3.3 million years ago
Size: 1 m (3 ft 3 in) tall
Diet: Omnivorous
Information: An offshoot from the hominid line, with a mixture of primitive (small ear holes) and advanced (flat face and small teeth).

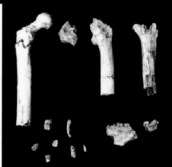

AUSTRALOPITHECUS

Meaning: Southern ape
Time: Pliocene to Pleistocene
Size: 1 m (3 ft 3 in) tall
Diet: Omnivorous
Information: The most important of our immediate ancestors. Consisting of several species, one of which would have been our direct ancestor.

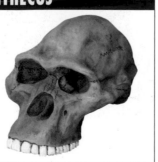

Homo habilis

Time: Pliocene. 2.3-1.6 million years ago

Diet: Omnivorous

Habitat: Open grassland

Information: A toolmaker and contemporary of *Australopithecus africanus*.

Homo erectus

Time: Pleistocene. 1.8-0.3 million years ago

Diet: Omnivorous

Habitat: All over the place

Information: The earliest widespread species, from France to Java, representing the move from Africa.

Homo ergaster

Time: Pliocene. 1.8-1.2 million years ago

Diet: Omnivorous

Habitat: Open grassland

Information: Very similar to *Homo erectus*, but confined to Africa.

Homo heidelbergensis

Time: Pleistocene. 0.5-0.2 million years ago

Diet: Omnivorous

Habitat: Open grassland

Information: Intermediate between *Homo erectus* and *Homo sapiens* and sometimes classed as one or the other.

Our epic film has brought us up until the present day, but the film has not ended. The events of the past did not just happen to reach the present day. Although we like to think that the Earth's history has happened so that humans can exist, humans are just another step in the development of life. Progress will continue, and the exciting drama of life on Earth will continue as long as the Earth itself exists. Who knows what exciting events could happen on Earth in future years to come.

OUT OF THE CRADLE

All the early evolution of hominids took place in Africa. It was with the development of *Homo erectus* that they left this continent and spread through Europe and Asia.
Then, evolving into *Homo sapiens*, they crossed into -

Australia	65,000 years ago
North America	50,000 years ago
South America	12,500 years ago
Moon	1969

Dmanisi
1.6 mya

Lantian
800,000

Zhoukoudian
500,000

Central Europe
730,000

Koobi Fora
1.8 mya

Sangiran
1.6 mya

Morokeyto
1.8 mya

THE DEVELOPMENT OF CULTURE AND CIVILIZATION

Things that we take for granted in civilized
life developed over a long period of time,
and in different places at different times.

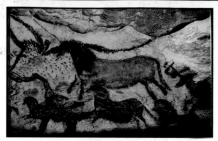

Neolithic (new stone age)
Development of agriculture, everywhere 9,000-1,800 years ago

Hunting weapons, North America 11,000 years ago

Upper Palaeolithic (old stone age)
Cave art, France 33,000 years ago

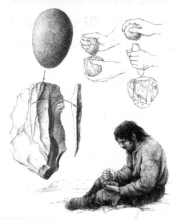

Lower Palaeolithic
Complex flake tools, France 100,000-40,000 years ago

Simple flake tools, Britain and France 450,000-100,000 years ago

Stone tools, everywhere 2.5-1.5 million years ago

HOMO

Time: Pliocene to recent
Size: 1.8 m (5 ft 9 in) tall

Diet: Omnivorous
Information: The modern human

being. Several species developed,
but only one survives.

ANIMAL PROFILES

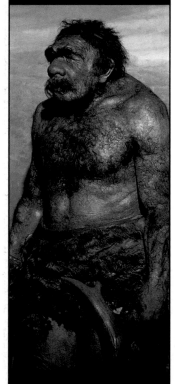

Homo neanderthalensis

Time: Peistocene. 250,000-
30,000 years ago

Diet: Omnivorous

Habitat: Cold conditions

Information: Neanderthal
man, and often regarded
as a subspecies of
Homo sapiens.

Homo floriensis

Time: Pliocene. 18,000
years ago

Diet: Omnivorous

Habitat: Forested islands

Information: A dwarf
species about 1 metre
(3 ft 3 in) tall, nicknamed
"the Hobbit".

Homo sapiens

Time: Pleistocene to
recent. 100,000 years
ago to now

Diet: Omnivorous

Habitat: Everywhere

Information: You and I.

UNCOVERING THE PREHISTORIC WORLD

The way we know about the history of life on Earth is through the detailed accumulation of little bits of knowledge built up over the centuries by visionary and hard-working scientists. A list such as this cannot be exhaustive. There are many others whose contributions were as great but just did not make it on to this page because of lack of room.

TIMELINE OF THE HISTORY OF GEOLOGY AND PALAEONTOLOGY

610-425 BC Philosophers Thales, Anaximander, Pythagoras, Xenophanes and Herodotus recognize that fossils show that the distribution of land and sea was once different.

Calcite – a common mineral

78 BC Pliny the Elder writes the first natural history encyclopaedia.

c.1000 AD Al-Beruni (973-1050) observes that different grades of sediment is deposited by different strengths of river currents – an early observation of sedimentology. He also puts precious minerals in their geological context.

1020 Avicenna (or Sina) observes the work of erosion.

1056 Albertus Magnus publishes a book on minerals.

1500 Leonardo da Vinci (1452-1519) states that fossils are remains of animals and their enclosing rocks must have been lifted from below sea level.

1542 Leonhart Fuchs publishes a catalogue of 500 plant species.

1546 Georgius Agricola (born George Bauer, 1494-1555) "Father of mineralogy" classifies minerals by their crystal shape and composition. Publishes an analysis of ore bodies.

1585 Michele Mercati opens the first geological museum.

1596 Dutch cartographer Abraham Ortelius first suggests continental drift.

1600 William Gilbert, Elizabeth I's physician, describes the Earth's magnetism.

1616 Italian philosopher Lucilio Vanini first to suggest humans descended from apes; he was executed.

1641 Lawyer Isaac La Peyrère suggests that people existed before Adam and Eve. His ideas were only published after his death.

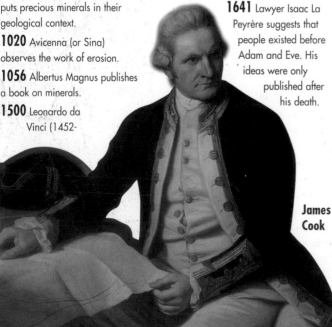

James Cook

1658 Jesuit missionary Martino Martini shows that Chinese history predates the above. Nobody takes notice.

1668 Robert Hooke claims that the Earth's movements and not the biblical Flood, moved fossils to dry land.

1669 Nicolaus Steno (born Neils Stensen, 1638-86) establishes the laws of stratigraphy, which state that rock beds laid down horizontally, stacked on one another and subsequently contorted.

1679 Scandinavian historian Olof Rudbeck tries to date sedimentary rocks.

1688 The Ashmolean Museum opens in Oxford – the world's first public museum.

1715 Edmund Halley suggests the age of the Earth can be calculated from the salinity of the seas.

1735 Linnaeus establishes the binomial classification of living things.

1745 Mikhail Vasil'evich Lomonosov (1711-65) recognizes that ancient geological processes would have been similar to today's, in anticipation of James Hutton (see below).

1749 Georges-Louis Leclerc de Buffon speculates that the planets formed by a comet crashing into the sun. The people in power force him to retract.

1751 Diderot and d'Alembert publish the first encyclopaedia – with a reliance on factual information rather than on traditional wisdom.

1760 Giovanni Arduino classifies the geological column – Primary: with no fossils, Secondary: deformed and with fossils, Tertiary: horizontal and with fossils, and Quaternary: loose sands and gravels over the rest. This was coarse but the basis of modern classification.

1766 Torbern Olaf Bergman (1735-1784) sees that different rock types were formed at different times, and appreciates the organic origin of fossils.

1768 James Cook's voyage brings an awareness of the range of plants and animals around the world to the United Kingdom.

1771 Joseph Priestley discovers

The Earth's magnetism

oxygen and shows its importance to life.

1778 Buffon puts the age of the Earth at 74,832 years.

1789 French researcher Antoine Lavoisier interprets different sedimentary rocks as showing different sea levels in the past.

1795 James Hutton "Founder of modern geology" sees geological processes as a cycle, with no beginning and no end.

1799 Alexander von Humboldt names the Jurassic system.

1799 British surveyor William Smith produces the first geological map, establishing the importance of fossils to define rocks and times.

1804 Cuvier acknowledges that fossil animals are older than can be explained by the Bible, suggests previous cycles of creation and destruction.

1824 Buckland describes the first

Alfred Wegener

dinosaur.

1830 Charles Lyell publishes his influential *Principles of Geology*.

1837 Charles Darwin uses natural selection to explain evolution, but the idea is not published until 1859.

1837 Swiss scientist Louis Agassiz detects the Ice Age.

1841 William Smith's nephew John Phillips names geological eras Palaeozoic, Mesozoic and Cenozoic.

1842 Sir Richard Owen invents the term "dinosaur".

1848 Science magazine established by the American Association for the Advancement of Science.

1866 Austrian monk Gregor Mendel establishes the laws of heredity. His work remains unknown until about 1900.

1871 Darwin publishes *The Descent of Man*.

1894 Eugene Debois describes *Pithecanthus erectus* (now *Homo erectus*) as the missing link between humans and apes.

1902 Walter Sutton discovers the chromosome theory of inheritance.

1902 Physicist Ernest Rutherford shows that radioactivity means that the Earth is older than Kelvin said.

1912 Alfred Wegener proposes continental drift.

1927 Belgian priest Georges Lemaître proposed that the universe began with the explosion of a primeval atom – a forerunner of the Big Bang theory.

1934 American geologist Charles F. Richter establishes the Richter scale for measuring earthquakes.

1946 Geologist Reg Sprigg finds the oldest fossils of multicellular organisms in Australia.

1953 Stanley Miller and Harold Urey

Crick and Watson

combine the gases of the Earth's initial atmosphere and form the chemicals from which living things are made.

1953 James Watson and Francis Crick determine the molecular structure of DNA.

1953 Fiesel Houtermans and Claire Patterson use radiometric dating to date the Earth at 4.5 billion years.

1956 Keith Runcorn notes polar wandering based on palaeomagnetic studies.

1961 Amateur meteorologist GS

Darwin studied the features of different species to develop his theory of evolution.

Callander notes the rise in greenhouse gases in the atmosphere and warns of a global warming.

1963 Fred Vine and Drummond Matthews discover seafloor spreading. This leads to the establishment of plate tectonics.

1964 Arno Penzias and Robert Wilson detect cosmic radiation and use it to confirm the Big Bang Theory.

1966 Willi Hennig develops cladistics, a new approach to studying evolutionary relationships.

1969 Moon rock samples prove that the moon the same age as the Earth.

1972 Stephen Jay Gould and Niles Eldredge develop the theory of punctuated equilibrium, meaning that evolution takes place in short bursts.

1974 John Ostrom resurrects the idea that birds evolved from dinosaurs – an idea that had been dormant for a century.

1980 Louis and Walter Alvarez put forward the asteroid impact theory of dinosaur extinction.

1985 Discovery by scientists of the British Antarctic Survey of the depletion of ozone in the upper atmosphere.

1988 Hottest northern hemisphere summer on record brings public awareness of global warming.

1991 Chicxulub crater in Yucatan is pinpointed as the site of the impact that may have caused the dinosaur extinction.

1992 Joe Kirschvink suggests the "snowball Earth" theory – that the Earth was covered by ice in Precambrian times.

A 50,000-year-old crater shows that the Earth is still being bombarded by meteors.

SOME WRONG DEDUCTIONS

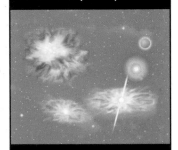

1650 Irish Archbishop Ussher calculates date of Creation at 4004 BC. This is widely accepted.

1780 Abraham Gottlob Werner (1749-1817) theorizes that all rocks are formed in ancient oceans. He is wrong but greatly influential.

1800 Lamarck proposes a theory of evolution. It suggested that traits that are acquired in life can be passed on to the next generation. This is no longer accepted since the general acceptance of Darwin's theory of natural selection.

1862 Lord Kelvin suggests that the Earth is 20–400 million years old, based on rates of cooling.

KEY FIGURES

SIR RICHARD OWEN

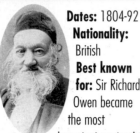

Dates: 1804-92
Nationality: British
Best known for: Sir Richard Owen became the most important anatomist of his day, determining that the way an animal lived could be deduced by its shape and the organs it possessed. However, he could not quite grasp the newly developed concept of evolution.
Key discoveries: Coined the term "dinosauria" in 1842 to encompass three new fossil animals recently discovered, from which we get the name "dinosaur".

WILLIAM BUCKLAND

Dates: 1784-1856
Nationality: British
Best known for: William Buckland was a lecturer and reader in geology at the University of Oxford. He toured Europe and established the basic principles of stratigraphic correlation, and became a scientific celebrity on his discovery of *Megalosaurus* and was the Dean of Westminster from 1845 to his death in 1857.
Key discoveries: *Megalosaurus*, the first dinosaur to be scientifically described.

WILLIAM SMITH

Dates: 1769-1839
Nationality: British
Best known for: William Smith observed the rocks of Britain in his role as a canal engineer, and realized that the same layers, or beds, of rocks could be traced over large areas by using their fossils to identify them. He eventually used this knowledge to compile the first ever geological map, in which mainland Britain was coloured according to the rock types.
Key discoveries: The principle of faunal succession, in which the same rocks can be identified by the fossils they contain, wherever they occur.

GEORGES CUVIER

Dates: 1769-1832
Nationality: French
Best known for: Georges Cuvier was one of the most influential figures in science of the time, particularly in the field of anatomy. He is regarded as the father of vertebrate palaeontology. He refused to acknowledge the fact of evolution and resisted the popularization or democratization of scientific knowledge.
Key discoveries: Classified all living and fossil things according to their similarity to one another, as we do today.

OTHNIEL CHARLES MARSH

Dates: 1831-99
Nationality: American
Best known for: Professor of palaeontology at Yale University and curator of the Peabody Museum of Natural History. Great rival of Edward Drinker Cope and their animosity resulted in the "bone wars" in which each tried to outdo the other in the number of dinosaurs discovered.
Key discoveries: About 80 new genera of dinosaurs, really establishing the vastness of fossil life.

CHARLES DARWIN

Dates: 1809-82
Nationality: British
Best known for: After failed attempts at careers in medicine and the church, he became a naturalist. His famous voyage on *HMS Beagle* allowed him to observe and collect examples of flora and fauna from all other the world. He built on the already existing ideas of evolution and deduced the mechanism involved.
Key discoveries: The idea of natural selection as the force that drives evolution.

EDWARD DRINKER COPE

Dates: 1840-97
Nationality: American
Best known for: Edward Drinker Cope was one of the first vertebrate palaeontologists in America and was affiliated to The Academy of Natural Sciences in Philadelphia. His arrogance drove him to fall out with Othniel Charles Marsh and this instigated the "bone wars". This event stimulated the discovery of dinosaurs, but drove more methodical workers away from the science.
Key discoveries: About 65 new dinosaur genera.

MARY ANNING

Dates: 1799-1847
Nationality: British
Best known for: Mary Anning was a professional fossil collector, working from the beaches of Dorset and Devon in the south of England. She began work when she was 12 years old to support her family after her father died. Mary Anning is credited with finding the first complete fossil at the age of just 12 on the beach of Lyme Regis. She supplied fossils for all the eminent scientists of the day.
Key discoveries: The first full skeleton of an ichthyosaur and also of the first plesiosaur.

See page 30 -31 for more information on ichthyosaurs.

LOUIS SEYMOUR BAZETT LEAKEY

Dates: 1903-72
Nationality: British/Kenyan
Best known for: Louis Seymour Bazett Leakey was born in Kenya. He became an archaeologist and tried to prove Darwin's theory that humans evolved in Africa. He succeeded. His most significant work was done in Olduvai Gorge in Tanzania where he found evidence of early tool-using.
Key discoveries: Various species of *Australopithecus*, but given different names at the time.

CHARLES DOOLITTLE WALCOTT

Dates: 1850-1927
Nationality: American
Best known for: Walcott worked for, and became the director of, the US Geological Survey. He was a vertebrate palaeontologist and worked mostly in the Cambrian of the United Sates and Canada. He later became the Secretary of the Smithsonian Institution and was one of the most powerful figures in the American scientific community.
Key discoveries: The discovery of the Burgess Shale and its variety of fantastic Cambrian fossils.

ALFRED WEGENER

Dates: 1880-1930
Nationality: German
Best known for: Alfred Wegener was a meteorologist, doing a great deal of work in Greenland. He advocated the concept of continental drift (calling it "continental displacement" when he first lectured on it in 1912), although he could not think of a mechanism that would account for the phenomenon. He died in an accident on the Greenland ice cap.
Key discoveries: Proposing continental drift as a serious scientific idea.

SIR CHARLES LYELL

Dates: 1797-1875
Nationality: British
Best known for: Sir Charles Lyell was a field geologist who published a ground-breaking work *The Principles of Geology* in which he explained the observed geological phenomena in terms of scientific actions rather than the works of God. He stressed that the human species must have been older than currently believed.
Key discoveries: Establishing the geological column, with time divided into periods.

PALAEONTOLOGY

Fossils, the remains of life of the past, have been found just about everywhere there are deposits of sedimentary rocks. Dinosaurs; the spectacular and popular inhabitants of the past world, are a very rare part of this fossil treasure trove. Nevertheless, they have been found on all the continents of the Earth. Excavation of their remains is a very specialist task carried out by experts called palaeontologists.

DINOSAURS ALL AROUND THE WORLD

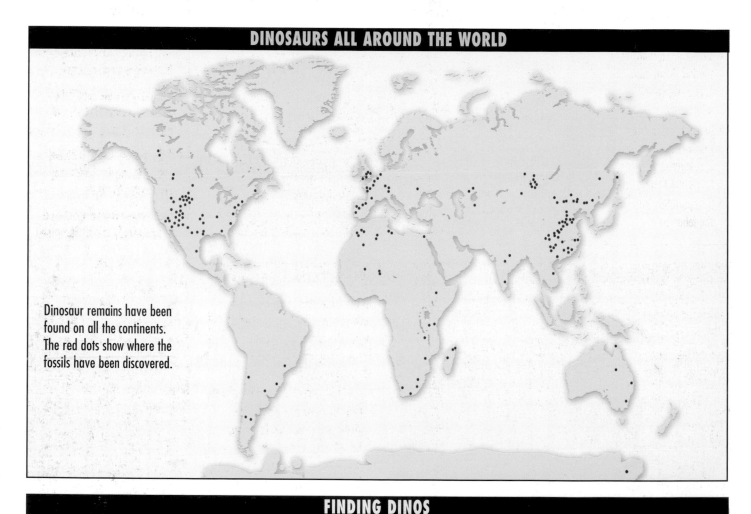

Dinosaur remains have been found on all the continents. The red dots show where the fossils have been discovered.

FINDING DINOS

Dinosaur remains are found:

- By chance – where walkers see a fossil sticking out from a cliff face, or where builders or quarry workers come across them during their work. Because of the surface of the Earth's continuous change, these exposures are more common than you might think.

- By scientific expedition – where scientists investigate a certain region with exposures of the right types of rocks.

See pages 12-13 for more information on fossils.

Chance exposures result from:

- Erosion by wind in the desert, where the rock is exposed and uncluttered by soil or vegetation.

- In eroded rubble where loose material has fallen from a cliff face. It may be difficult to trace the specimen back to its original bedrock.

- Where rivers have carved out gorges in the landscape.

EXCAVATION AND TRANSPORTATION

Once found, a dinosaur skeleton is excavated using the following techniques:

- Removing the overburden: Taking off the layers of rock above it to reveal the whole thing.
- Mapping: Plotting where the individual bones lie. This is important in later study.

- Jacketing: Sealing the bones in a layer of plaster to protect them.
- Transportation back to the laboratory.

DINO DISPLAYS

If the skeleton is for public display, it is not usually the original that is used but a cast. To create the cast, the following process is carried out:

- A mould is made of each bone of the skeleton.
- A reproduction of the bone is cast in glass fibre or some other lightweight tough material.
- Missing bones are supplied as casts from other skeletons of the same animal.
- If there is no original material available, missing bones may be sculpted by artists.
- The skeleton is assembled on a frame, usually in a lifelike pose.

IN THE LAB

In the laboratory, specialist technicians called preparators make the specimens ready for study by the scientists. They do this by:

- Removing the plaster jacket.
- Removing any adhering matrix — the rock in which the fossil was buried — with fine tools.
- Sometimes separating the bones by dissolving the matrix in an acid bath.
- Hardening delicate bone fossils by coating them with shellac or some other varnish.

MUSEUMS WITH GOOD DINOSAUR COLLECTIONS

AFRICA

Bernard Price Institute of Palaeontology, Johannesburg.

Museum of Earth Sciences, Rabat

ASIA

Museum of the Institute of Vertebrate Palaeontology and Palaeoanthropology, Beijing.

Academy of Sciences, Ulan-Bator.

National Science Museum, Tokyo

AUSTRALIA

Queensland Museum, Fortitude Valley, Queensland.

EUROPE

The Natural History Museum, London.

Royal Institute of Natural Sciences, Brussels.

Natural History Museum, Humboldt University, Berlin.

Palaeontological Institute, Moscow.

NORTH AMERICA

Tyrrell Museum of Palaeontology, Drumheller, Alberta.

American Museum of Natural History, New York.

National Museum of Natural

History, Smithsonian Institution, Washington, D.C.

Field Museum of Natural History, Chicago.

SOUTH AMERICA

Argentine Museum of Natural Sciences, Buenos Aires.

Museum of La Plata University, La Plata.

GLOSSARY

Algae Simple, non-flowering plants which usually grow in water.

Ammonite An extinct marine mollusc with a flat-coiled spiral shell, found as fossils chiefly in Jurassic and Cretaceous deposits.

Anthracite A hard variety of coal that contains relatively pure carbon.

Archaeology The study of human history and prehistory through the excavation of sites and the analysis of physical remains.

Arthropod An invertebrate animal that has a segmented body, external skeleton and jointed limbs.

Atmosphere The layer of enveloping gases which surround the Earth.

Binomial classification The classification of living things in which animals and plants are given two names – a genus name and a species name. For example *Homo sapiens* or *Tyrannosaurus rex*. This is useful when discussing various species of the same genus, such as *Homo sapiens*, *Homo erectus* or *Homo ergaster*. Usually only the genus name, *Tyrannosaurus* or *Homo*, is used. Sometimes in a text, when the full name has already been given, then the genus name can be

abbreviated to its initial – hence *T. rex*. The genus name always takes a capital initial but the species name does not, and both are given in italics.

Biped An animal which walks on two feet.

Carnivore An animal that feeds on meat.

Chert A hard, dark, opaque rock composed of silica with a microscopically fine-grained texture.

Club moss A member of a primitive group of plants, related to the ferns. Modern types are low herbaceous forms, but in the late Palaeozoic they grew tree-sized and formed forests.

Coal A combustible black rock consisting mainly of carbonized plant matter and used as fuel.

Conifer A tree bearing cones and evergreen needle-like or scale-like leaves.

Continent Any of the world's main continuous expanses of land, usually consisting of an ancient core and surrounded by successively younger mountain ranges.

Creodont A carnivorous mammal of the early Tertiary period.

Crystal A piece of a solid substance having a natural geometrically regular form with symmetrically arranged faces.

Diagenesis The physical and chemical changes occurring during the conversion of sediment to sedimentary rock.

Eon The largest division of geological time. It comprises several eras.

Era A division of geological time, smaller than an eon but larger than a period. Typically an

era lasts for hundreds of millions of years, and encompasses several periods. For example the Mesozoic era comprises the Triassic, Jurassic and Cretaceous periods.

Erosion A gradual wearing away of rocks or soil.

Eukaryote A living cell that carries its genetic material in a well-defined nucleus. Most living things nowadays are composed of eukaryotic cells.

Evolution The development of different kinds of living organisms from earlier forms.

Excavation The careful removal of earth from an area in order to find buried remains.

Facies A term that geologists use to cover everything about a rock or a sequence of rocks – its derivation, its fossils, its colour, its age, the landform produced – in fact everything that makes the rock distinctive.

Fauna The animals of a particular region, habitat or geological period.

Fern A flowerless plant which has feathery or leafy fronds.

Flora The plants of a particular region, habitat or geological period.

Fossil The remains or impression of a prehistoric plant or animal embedded in rock and preserved.

Geology The study of the Earth, how it is made and how it evolved.

Glaciated Covered or having been covered by glaciers or ice sheets.

Graptolite A planktonic invertebrate animal.

Herbivore An animal which eats only plants.

Hinterland The remote areas of a country, away from the coast or the banks of major rivers.

Hominid The group of animals to which humans belong.

Ice Age A period of time when climates were cooler than they are now and glaciers were more extensive.

Ichthyosaur One of a group of swimming reptiles from the Mesozoic. They had streamlined fish-like bodies and tail fins.

Igneous Rock solidified from lava or magma.

Isthmus A narrow strip of land with sea on either side, linking two larger areas of land.

Landmass A continent or other large body of land.

Latitude The angular distance of a place north or south of the equator.

Lava Hot molten or semi-fluid rock erupted from a volcano or fissure, or solid rock resulting from cooling of this.

Magma Hot fluid or semi-fluid material within the Earth's crust from which lava and other igneous rock is formed by cooling.

Marginocephalians A group of dinosaurs with armoured heads. They consisted of the pachycephalosaurids, like *Stygimoloch*, and the ceratopsians, like *Triceratops*.

Mass extinction An event that brings about the extinction of a large number of animals and plants. There have been about five mass extinctions in the history of life on Earth.

Metamorphic Rock that has undergone transformation by heat, pressure, or other natural processes without actually melting.

Meteorite A piece of rock from space.

Mineral A naturally-formed inorganic substance with a specific chemical composition. Minerals are the building bricks of rocks.

Molecule A group of atoms bonded together.

Mosasaur A member of a group of big swimming reptiles of the Cretaceous period, closely related to modern monitor lizards.

Mucus A slimy substance secreted by the mucus membrances and glands of animals for lubrication and protection.

Omnivore An animal which eats both plants and meat.

Organ A structure in a living body that carries out a particular function. Organs are made up of tissues.

Organism An individual animal, plant, or single-celled life form.

Palaeo- As a prefix this means something ancient. Note that, in America, words incorporating "palaeo-" omit the "a", resulting in "Paleontology, Paleozoic, Paleocene", etc.

Palaeontology The study of ancient life and fossils.

Peat Partly decomposed vegetable matter forming a deposit on acidic, boggy ground. It is dried for use in gardening and as fuel.

Period A division of geological time that can be defined by the types of animals or plants that existed then. Typically a period lasts for tens of millions of years, and is further sub-divided into sub–periods, epochs, sub-epochs and then stages.

Petrify To change organic matter into stone by encrusting or replacing its original substance with a mineral deposit.

Phenomenon A fact or situation that is observed to exist or happen, especially the existence of something which is in question.

Plankton The tiny animal and plant life that drifts in the waters of the ocean.

Plate tectonics The process whereby the surface of the Earth is continually being created and destroyed – new material being formed along ocean ridges and old material being lost down ocean trenches. The movement involved causes the continents to travel over the Earth's surface.

Plesiosaur A large fossil marine reptile of the Mesozoic era, with large, paddle-like limbs and a long flexible neck.

Pliosaur A plesiosaur with a short neck, large head and massive toothed jaws.

Pterosaur One of a group of flying reptiles from the Mesozoic. They flew with leathery wings supported by an elongate finger, *Pterodactylus* was a pterosaur.

Radioactivity The process in which an atom of a particular element breaks down to form another element. This process is accompanied by a release of energy which is the basis of nuclear power.

Reef A ridge on the sea bed giving rise to shallow water.

Most reefs are formed from the remains of living creatures.

Rift valley A steep-sided valley formed by subsidence of the Earth's surface between nearly parallel faults.

Rock A naturally formed inorganic substance that makes up the Earth. A typical rock will be made of several types of mineral.

Silica A hard, unreactive, colourless compound which occurs as quartz and as the principal constituent of sandstone and other rocks.

Salinity The amount of salt dissolved in sea water.

Sediment Matter carried by water or wind and deposited on the land surface or seabed.

Sedimentary Rock that has formed from sediment deposited by water or wind.

Sedimentology The aspect of geology that deals with the deposition of sand and silt and other sediments before becoming sedimentary rocks.

Seismic Of or relating to earthquakes or other vibrations of the Earth and its crust.

Shingle A mass of small rounded pebbles, especially on a seashore.

Stratigraphy The aspect of geology that deals with the sequence of deposition of rocks, their structures and fossils, and interprets them to find out about conditions of former times.

Taphonomy The study of what happens to a dead organism before it becomes a fossil.

Tectonics Large-scale processes affecting the structure of the Earth's crust.

Thyreophorans A group of dinosaurs that carried armour. They consisted of the plated stegosaurs, like *Stegosaurus*, and the armoured ankylosaurs, like *Euoplocephalus*.

Tissue The living substance of a body. Tissue is made up of cells, and is the substance from which organs are built.

Trilobite A segmented arthropod, common in Palaeozoic seas.

Vertebrate An animal with a backbone.

Volcano A mountain or hill having a crater or vent through which lava, rock fragments, hot vapour and gas are or have been erupted from the Earth's crust.

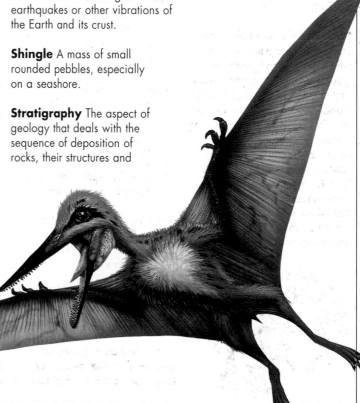

INDEX

The letters a, b, c, d, following the page number indicate the column (lettering from left to right) in which the information may be found on that page.

A

abelisaurs 37d
Adam and Eve 52b
aerial creatures 31a-c
Agassiz, Louis 53a
Age of Fishes 18a
Age of Reptiles 26a
Agricola, Georgius (George Bauer) 52b
Al-Beruni 52a
Alamosaurus 36a
Albertus Magnus 52a
Alembert, Jean le Rond d' 52c
Aleutian Islands 9b-d
algae 14b-d, 22a-d
Alticamelus 44a
Alvarez, Louis and Walter 53c
amber 12a
Ambulocetus 42a
American Association for the Advancement of Science 53a
ammonites 29d
amphibians 18b-d, 21a-c, 21d, 26a, 41a-c
Anatotitan 38a
Anaximander 52a
Andes Mountains 9b-d
andesite 10d
animals 12, 18b-d, 21a-c, 21d, 23d, 52d, 54a
    Burgess Shale 17a-c
    cold-adapted 47a-c
    Early Tertiary 42b-d
    land-living 31a-c, 40a
    sea-living 22a, 28a, 30a-d, 31a-c
    Triassic period 26, 27
Anisian stage 24a
ankylosaurids 39a, 39d
ankylosaurs 32b, 38a, 39a
Ankylosaurus 39d
Anning, Mary 55b
Anomalocaris 17c
anthracite 20a-d
Apatosaurus 33d
Apex Chert, Australia 14a
Arambourg, Camille 35a-c
Arambourgiania 35a-c
Archaean era 6-7b, 14a
Archaeoceratops 39d
Archaeopteryx 31d
Archelon 35d
Ardipithecus 49c
Ardipithecus ramidus 48b-d
Arduino, Giovanni 52c
Argentinasaurus 36a
armadilloes 47d
Arthroplura 21d
arthropods 17a, 21a-c
Artinskian stage 22a
Ashmolean Museum, Oxford 52c
Asselian stage 22a
Atlantic Ocean 8, 8a, 28b-d
Atlantis, US 8a
atmosphere 18b-d, 25d, 53b
Austalopithecus bahrelghazali 48a
Australopithecus 49a-b, 55c-d
Australopithecus aethiopicus 48b-d, 49d
Australopithecus afarensis 48a
Australopithecus africanus 48a, 50a
Australopithecus anamensis 48a
Australopithecus bahrelghazali 48a
Australopithecus boisei 48b-d, 49d
Australopithecus garhi 49d
Australopithecus robustus 48b-d, 49d
Avicenna 52a
Azores 8b-c

B

Bacon, Francis 8a
bacteria 14b-d
Bala sub-period 16a
Baryonyx 36a
basalt 10c, 14a, 41d
Bashkirian epoch 20a
bats 43d
beaches, raised 47a-c
Beagle, HMS 54c-d
belemnites 30
Bergman, Torbern Olaf 52d
Bible, age of Earth 6-7e
Big Bang theory 53b, 53c
binomial classification 52c
biogenic rocks 10c
Birch 38b-d
birds 31d, 36b-d, 41a-c, 42b-d, 43a, 53c
Bitter Springs Chert, Australia 14a
bituminous coal 20a-d
bivalves 22a-d
Bothriolepis 19d
brachiopods 22a-d
brachiosaurs 36a
Brachiosaurus 33d
British Antarctic Survey 53c
Brontotherium 43b-c
Buckland, William 53a, 54b-d
Buffon, George-Louis Leclerc de 52c, 52d
Bunter 24b-d
Burgess Shale 17a-d, 55c-d
Buxolestes 43d

C

Calamites 21b-c
calcite 29a-c, 52a
Callander, GS 53c
Calymene 17a-c
Cambrian period 16a, 16b-d
camels 44a
Canadian sub-period 16a
Capitanian stage 22a
Carboniferous period 6-7d, 10-21, 16a
Carnian stage 24a
Carnotaurus 37a-c
casts 12b-c
cats 44a
Caudipteryx 36b-d
Cenozoic era 6-7c
centipedes 21a-c
Cephalaspis 19a-c
ceratopsians 39b-c
Ceratosaurus 33d
chalk 24b-d, 34a-b
Changxingian stage 22a
Charnodiscus 15b
chemical rocks 10c, 11b
chert 14a
Chicxulub crater, Yucatan 40b-d, 41a-c, 52a, 53c
Chriacus 43d
chromosomes 53b
cladistics 53c
Cladoselache 19d
classification 54a
clastic rocks 10c, 11a, 11b
clay 11b
climate
    change 25d, 40b-d, 41a-c, 44b-d

cooling 44b-d, 45c
  Triassic 25a-d
Climatius 19d
coal 6-7d, 11b, 12a, 20a-d
coal forests 6-7d, 21a-c,
  22b-d, 25a-c
Coelodonta 47d
Columbus, Christopher 8
comet strike 40b-d
Compsognathus 33d
conglomerates 11a, 29a-c
conifers 21c, 25a-c, 26b-d, 39a
continental drift 8, 52b, 55a-b
continental shelves 30a-d
continents 14b-d
Cook, James 52a-b, 52c, 52d
Cope, Edward Drinker 54b, 55a
corals 22a-d, 31a-c
cordaites 21c, 25a-c
Corythosaurus 38a
Cranioceras 44a
Crassigyrinus 21d
creodonts 43b-c
Cretaceous period 6-7d, 24a,
  34-5, 40, 41a-c
Crick, Francis 53b
crinoids 22a-d
crocodiles 27d, 31d, 35d,
  41a-c.30a-d
Cryptoclidus 30a-d
Cryptolithus 17d
crystals 10a, 10b, 11d
Cuvier, Georges 52d, 54a
cycads 39a

D
Daphoneus 45d
Darwin, Charles 53a, 53c,
  53d, 54c-d
death assemblage 13c-d
Debois, Eugene 53a
Deccan Trapps 41d
deer 45a-c
Deinosuchus 35d
Deinotherium 45a-b
deserts 22a, 22b-d, 24b-d,
  28b-d
Devonian period 6-7, 16a,
  18-19
diagenesis 13b
Diatryma 43a
Diderot, Denis 52c
Didymograptus 17a-c

Dimetrodon 23a-c
Dimylus 45d
dinosaurs 6-7d, 26, 27, 28a,
  28b-d, 34, 36b-d, 38a,
  38b-d, 41a-c, 42b-d, 53a,
  54a, 54b, 55a, 56-7
  Cretaceous 32a
  eggshells 41a-c
  extinction 53c
  footprints 12c
  Jurassic 28b-d, 32-3
  museums 57
  Triassic 26, 27
Diplodocus 33a-c, 33d,
Diplograptus 17a-c
Diplovertebron 21d
Diprodoton 47d
Dirac, PAM 9a
disease 40a, 40b-d, 41a-c
DNA 53b
dogs 45d
dolerite 10b
dolphins 45d
duckbills 38a, 39b-c
ducks 43d
dune bedding 22a
Dunkleosteus 19d
Dyfed sub-period 16a

E
Early Palaeozoic period 6-7d,
  16-17, 16a, 16b-d
Early Tertiary period 6-7d, 42-3
Earth
  age 6-7e, 52d, 53c, 53d
  cross section 9
  expansion 9a
  magnetism 8b, 52d
  see also world
earthquakes 53b
East African Rift Valley 9b-d
Edmontonia 39d
Eifelian stage 18a
elasmosaurs 35a-c
Elasmosaurus 35a-c
Eldredge, Niles 53c
elephants 45a-b, 45d
Elephas Primigenius 47a-b
elk 47d
Emsian stage 18a
encylopaedias 52a, 52c
Eocene epoch 42a
Eodiscus 17d

Eogyrinus 21a-c
Eoraptor 27a-b
Epigaulus 45d
erosion 52a
Eryops 23d
Erythrosuchus 27d
Eudimorphodon 27c
eukaryotes 15b
Euoplocephalus 39a
Eurhinodelphis 45d
Eusthenopteron 19a-c
evaporates 29a-c
evolution 53a, 53d, 54a, 54c-d
extrusive rocks 10b, 10c, 10d

F
Famennian stage 18a
faunal succession 54b-d
ferns 18a, 21c, 24a, 25a-c,
  26b-d
fish 18a, 18b-d, 19a-c, 19d,
  31d, 41a-c
forests 6-7d
fossils 11d, 12-13, 14b-d, 16a,
  30, 52a, 52b, 52c, 54b-d,
  55b, 56
  facies 12d
  gunflint chert microfossils 14a
  index 12d, 29d, 38a, 39b-c
  lagoons 31a-c
  trace 12c, 16a
Frasnian stage 18a
Fuchs, Leonhart 52b
fuel 29a-c

G
gabbro 10b
Gallic sub-epoch 34a
geological classification 52c
geological column/time scale
  6-7d-e, 55c-d
geological maps 52d, 54b-d
geological museums 52b
geological processes 52c, 52d
Gilbert, William 52b
giraffes 45a-c
Givetian stage 18a
glacials and glaciation 15b,
  46b-d, 47a-c
glaciers 46a-c
global warming 25a-d, 53c
Glossopteris 24a
Glyptodon 47d

gneiss 11d
Gondwana 34b-d
Goodchild, JG 6-7e
Gould, Stephen Jay 53c
granite 10b
graptolites 17a-c
grass and grasslands 44b-d
Great Extinction 6-7d, 40-1
greenhouse effect 40b-d, 53c
Griesbachian stage 24a
Gulf epoch 34a
Gzelian epoch 20a

H
Hadean era 6-7b, 14a
halite/rock salt 11b
Halley, Edmund 52c
Hallucigenia 17c
Haughton, Samuel 6-7e
Hawaii 10c
Hennig, Willi 53c
heredity 53a
Herodotus 52a
Hess, Harry 8a, 8c
Hettangian age 28a
Hilgenberg, OW 9a
Holocene epoch 46a
hominids 50b-d
Homo 50-1
Homo erectus 48b-d, 50a, 53a
Homo ergaster 50a
Homo florienses 51d
Homo habilis 48b-d, 50a
Homo heidelbergensis 50a

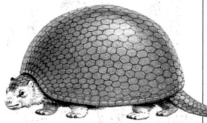

Homo neanderthalensis 51d
Homo rudolfensis 48b-d
Homo sapiens 48b-d, 50a, 51d
Hooke, Robert 52c
horns 45a-c
horses 43a-c, 44a
horsetails 18a, 21b, 25a-c
Houtermans, Fiesel 53b
humans 48-9, 52b
Humboldt, Alexander von 28a-d, 52d
Hutton, James 52c, 52d
Hylonomus 21d
Hyperodapedon 27d
Hypsodus 43d
Hyracotherium 43a-c

I

Icaronycteris 43d
Ice ages 16b-d, 22b-d, 43a, 46a, 46d, 53a
Iceland 10c
ichthyosaurs 27d, 29d, 30a-d, 31d, 35a-c, 55b
Ichthyosaurus 29d
Ichthyostega 19a-c
igneous rocks 10, 11a-c
Iguanodon 38a, 39b-c
India 41d
Indricotherium 42a
inheritance 53b
insectivores 42a, 45d
insects 6-7d, 12a, 18b-d
intrusive rocks 10a, 10b

iridium 40b-d, 41d
iron 19a-c
Isotelus 17d

J

jellyfish 15b
Joly, John 6-7e
Jura Mountains 28a-d
Jurassic period 6-7, 24a, 28-31, 52d

K

Kasimovian epoch 20a
Kelvin, William Thomson, Lord 6-7e, 53b, 53d
Kentrosaurus 33d
Kenyanthropus 49a-b
kettle holes 47a-c
Keuper 24b-d
Kimmeridgian stage 28a
Kirschvink, Joe 53c
Kronosaurus 35a-c
Kungurian stage 22a

L

La Peyrère, Isaac 52b
Ladinian stage 24a
Lamarck, Jean 53d
land bridges 40a
landmasses 14b-d, 16b-d
Late Proterozoic era 14b-d
Late Tertiary period 44-5
lava 10b, 11a-c
Lavoisier, Antoine 52d
Leakey, Louis Seymour Bazett 55c-d
Leedsihcthys 31d
Lemaître, Georges 53b
Leonardo da Vinci 52a-b
Lepidodendron 21a-b
Leptictidium 42a
lias 29a-c
Lias epoch 28a
life
    Cretaceous 36-7, 36-8
    Jurassic 30-3
    Precambrian 14a
    Triassic 26-7
    see also animals; dinosaurs; plants
life assemblage 13c-d
lignite 20a-d
limestone 11b, 11d, 15b, 24b-d,

29a-c, 31a-c, 34a-b
Linnaeus, Carolus 52c
Liopleurodon 31a-c
lithification 11a-c
lizards and snakes 41a-c
Llandovery epoch 16a
Lochkovian stage 18a
Lomonosov, Mikhail Vasil'evich 52c
Longtanian stage 22a
Lower Palaeolithic 51a-c
Ludlow epoch 16a
Lycaenops 23d
Lyell, Sir Charles 53a, 55c-d

M

Mackenzie Mountains, Canada 14a
Macrauchenia 47c
Magantereon 44a
magma 11a-c
magnetism 8b, 52b, 52d
Magnolia 38b-d
Malm epoch 28a
mammals 6-7d, 23a-c, 26, 42b-d, 43b-c, 44a
man 6-7d
marble 11d
Marella 17b
marginocephalians 32a
Mariana Trench 9b-d
marls 24b-d
Marsh, Othniel Charles 54b, 55a
marsupial mammals 41a-c, 45d
Martini, Martino 52c
Masiakasaurus 37d
mass extinctions 24b-d, 25d, 28a
Matthews, Drummond 8b, 53c
Mediterranean Sea 9b-d
Megaceros 47d
Megalania 47d
Megalosaurus 33d, 54b-d
Meganeura 21a-c
Megatherium 47a-b
Mendel, Gregor 53a
Mercati, Michele 52b
Mesoproterozoic period 14a
Mesosaurus 23a-c
Mesozoic era 6-7c, 24a, 27c, 27d, 40, 41a-c, 43a
metamorphic rocks 6-7b, 10c-d, 11a-c, 11d
meteor/ite impact 25d, 40a,

40b-d, 41a-c, 41d, 53c
meteorites 6-7b
Metriorhynchus 31d
microbes 14a
microfossils 14a
Mid-Atlantic Ridge 8b-c, 9b-d
Miller, Stanley 53b
millipedes 21d
minerals 6-7a, 10-11, 52a, 52b
Miocene epoch 42a
Mississippian sub-period 20a
Mixosaurus 27d
molecules 14b-d
Monograptus 17b
moon rock 53c
moraines 47a-c
Morley, Lawrence 8b
Morrison Formation 29a-c, 33a-c
mosasaurs 34c-d, 35a-c, 42b-d
Moschops 23d
Moscovian epoch 20a
mosses 21a-c, 25a-c
moulds 12b
Mount Saint Helens 10d
mountains 8d
mudstone 11a
multi-celled organisms 14a, 53b
Muschelkalk 24b-d

N

Nammalian stage 24a
natural selection 53d
Nectocaris 17b
Neocomian sub-epoch 34a
Neogene sub-period 42a, 43a
Neohipparion 44a
Neolithic (new stone age) 51a-c
Neoproterozoic period 14a
New Red Sandstone 22a, 22b-d, 24b-d
Newark Supergroup 29a-c
nodosaurid ankylosaurs 39d
nodosaurids 39a
Norian stage 24a
North America 8, 28b-d
North Atlantic 9a
Nothosaurus 27d

O

Oak 38b-d
oceanographic surveys 8a
oceans 14b-d

oil 12d, 19a-c, 22a-d
Old Red Sandstone 18b-d, 19a-c
Olenellus 17d
Oligocene epoch 42a
Oolitic limestone 29a-c
Opabinia 17b
Ophiderpeton 21d
Ophthalmosaurus 31d
Ordovician period 16a, 16b-d
ornithischians 32a, 32b, 36b-d, 38b-d
Ornithomimus 36a
ornithopods 32a
Orrorin 49a-b
Ortelius, Abraham 52b
ossicones 45a-c
Ostrom, John 53c
Ouranosaurus 38a
Oviraptor 37d
Owen, Sir Richard 53a, 54a
Oxfordian stage 28a
oxidisation 19a-c
Oxyaena 43b-c
oxygen 15c, 18c, 52d
ozone depletion 53c

P
Pacific Ocean 8b, 9a
Palaeocene epoch 42a
Palaeogene sub-period 42a, 43a
palaeomagnetic studies 53c
palaeontology 56-7
Palaeoparadoxia 44a
Palaeoproterozoic period 14a
Palaeozoic era 6-7c, 43a
Pangaea 24b-d, 25a-d, 28b-d, 31a-c, 34b-d
Panthalassa 24b-d
Parasaurolophus 39b-c
Pareiasaurus 23a-c
Patterson, Claire 53b
peat 20a-d
pebbles 22a
Pennsylvanian sub-period 20a
Penzias, Arno 53c
Permian period 6-7d, 16a, 22-3
petrified wood 12b
Phanerozoic eon 6-7c-e
Phillips, John 53a
Phorusrhacos 44b

Pithecanthus erectus (*Homo erectus*) 53a
placental mammals 41a-c
Placet, P 8a
planets 52c
plants 12, 52b, 52d
 coal forest 21a-c
 cold-adapted 47a-c
 Cretaceous 38-9
 Early Tertiary 42b-d
 land-living 16b, 18a, 18b-d
 Permian 25a-c
 Triassic 25a-c, 26b-d
plate tectonics 8-9, 11a-c, 13a, 53c
Platybelodon 45d
Pleistocene epoch 46a
Plesiadapis 43d
plesiosaurs 29d, 30a-d, 31a-c, 35a-c, 41a-c, 42b-d, 55b
Pleurosaurus 35d
Pliensbachian stage 28a
Pliny the Elder 52a
Pliocene epoch 42a
pliosaurs 29d, 30a-d, 31a-c, 35a-c
polacanthids 39a
Polacanthus 38a
polar wandering 53c
Pragian stage 18a
Precambrian eon 6-7a-b, 14-15, 43a
Presbyornis 43d
Pridoli epoch 16a
Priestley, Joseph 52d
Primary period 43a, 52c
primates 43d
 see also humans
Proceratops 36a
prokaryotes 15a
prosauropods 32a
Proterozoic era 6-7b, 14a
Psitticosaurus 39d
Pteranodon 35d
pterodactyloides 31a-c
Pterodactylus 31a-c
Pterodaustro 35d
pterosaurs 6-7d, 27c, 31a-c, 35a-c, 35d, 40, 42b-d
Pterosaurus 41a-c
punctuated equilibrium 53c
Pythagoras 52a

Q
quartz crystals 40b-d
Quaternary period 6-7, 43a, 46-7, 52c

R
radioactivity 6-7a-b, 6-7e, 53b
radiometric dating 53b
red sandstones 18, 19, 22, 24
Red Sea 9b-d, 14b-d
reefs 16b-d, 22a-d, 31a-c
Repenomamus 41d
reptiles 6-7d, 20a, 21a-c, 21d, 23a-c, 23d, 26a-d, 35d
 see also dinosaurs
Rhaetian stage 24a
rhinoceros 42a, 47d
Rhomaleosaurus 29d
rhynchosaurs 27d
Richter, Charles F 53b
rift valleys 28b-d
rock salt 11b
rocks 6-7a-b, 10-11, 24b-d, 53d
 cycle 11a-c
 Jurassic 29a-c
 see also types of rock
Rocky Mountains 28b-d, 33a-c
Rotliegendes epoch 22a
Rudbeck, Olaf 52c
Runcorn, Keith 53c
Rutherford, Ernest 53b

S
sabre-toothed tiger 47a-b
Sakmarian stage 22a
salinity, ocean 6-7e, 25d, 52c
salt *see* salinity
Saltasaurus 36b-d, 39a
sandstones 11a, 18, 19, 22, 24b-d, 29a-c
 Jurassic 29a-c
 Triassic 26a-d

saurischians 32a, 36b-d, 38b-d
sauropods 32a, 33a-c, 33d, 36a, 36b-d, 39a
Sauroposeidon 36a
schist 11d
Science magazine 53a
sea anemones 14a
sea levels 40a, 41a-c
sea lilies 22a-d
sea reptiles 35a-c, 40
sea scorpions 18b-d
seafloor spreading 8, 53c
Secondary 43a, 52c
sedimentary rocks 6-7a, 6-7e, 10, 11, 13a-d, 14a, 29a-c, 52c, 56
sedimentology 52a
sediments
 ocean 46b-d
 Tertiary 12a
seismic sea waves (tsunamis) 40b-d
Senonian sub-epoch 34a
Serpukhovian epoch 20a
Seymouria 23d
shales 11a, 11d, 29a-c
sharks 19d, 30a-d
shellfish 30
Siberia 22b-d
Sigillaria 21b
silica 14a, 44c-d
Silurian period 16a, 16b-d
Sinemurian stage 28a
Sinosauropteryx 37d
Sivatherium 45a-c
slate 11d
sloths 47a-b
Smilodon 47a-b

Smith, William 52d, 54b-d
snakes 41a-c
Snider, Antonio 8a
snowball Earth theory 15, 53c
Sollas 6-7e
South Australia 15b
Spathian stage 24a
Spinosaurus 37d
sponges 22a-d, 31a-c
Sprigg, Reg 53b
Spriggina 15b
stegosaurs 32b, 33d, 39a
Stegosaurus 33a-c
Steno, Nicolaus (Neils Stensen) 52c
stratigraphic correlation 54b-d
stratigraphy 52c
striations 47a-c
stromatolites 14b-d
Struthiosaurus 39d
Stygimoloch 38a
Styracosaurus 39d
Sutton, Walter 53b
Swaziland 14a
Synthetoceras 45a-b

T
T.Rex 6-7d
Tanystropheus 27d
Tapejara 35d
taphonomy 12a-d, 13a
Taylor, FB 8d
temperate woodland 41a-c
Tertiary period 6-7, 43a, 52c

Tethys Sea 31a-c
Thales 52a
Thecodontosaurus 27a-b
therizinosaurs 32a, 37a-c
Therizinosaurus 37a-c
theropods 32a, 33d, 36a, 36b-d, 37d
Thylacosmilus 45d
thyreophorans 32a, 33d
titanosaurs 36a
Tithonian stage 28a
Toarcian stage 28a
tortoises 41a-c
Tournaisian epoch 20a
tree ferns 25a-c
trees 25a-c
Triassic period 6-7d, 24-7
Triceratops 39b-c
trilobites 17a, 17b, 17d
Troodon 37d
tropical forest 41a-c
Tsintaosaurus 38a
tsunamis 40b-d
turtles 35d, 41a-c
Tylosaurus 34c-d
tyrannosaurs 37a-c
Tyrannosaurus 6-7d, 37a-c

U
Ufimian stage 22a
Uintatherium 42a
Upper Palaeolithic (old stone age) 51a-c
upright stance 49a-c

Ural Mountains 9b-d
Urey, Harold 53b
Ussher, Archbishop 53d

V
Vanini, Lucilio 52b
Velociraptor 37a-c
Vendian period 14a, 15
vertebrate palaeontology 54a, 55a, 55c-d
vertebrates 18b-d, 23a-c
Vesuvius 10d
Vine, Fred 8a, 53c
viruses 14b-d
Visean epoch 20a
volcanic activity 22b-d, 24b-d, 25d, 40b-d, 41a-c, 41d
volcanoes 10b, 10c
vulcanism *see* volcanic activity

W
Walcott, Charles Doolittle 6-7e, 17c, 55c-d
Watson, James 53b
Wegener, Alfred 8d, 53b, 55a-b
Wenlock epoch 16a
Werner, Abraham Gottlob 53d
Westlothiana 21a-c
whales 42a
Willow 38b-d
Wilson, Robert 53c
Wiwaxia 17b
wombat 47d
woolly mammoths 47a-b
Wordian stage 22a

world
Cambrian period 16b-d
Carboniferous period 20b-d
Cretaceous period 34b-d
Devonian period 18b-d
Early Tertiary period 42b-d
Jurassic period 28b-d
Late Tertiary period 44b-d
Ordovician period 16b-d
Permian period 22b-d
Quaternary period 46a-c
Silurian period 16b-d
Triassic period 24b-d
see also Earth
worms 15b

X
Xenophanes 52a

Y
Yucatan 40b-d, 41a-c, 52a

Z
Zechstein epoch 22a